LETTER
to an
IMAGINARY
FRIEND
PARTS
I & II

Books by Thomas McGrath

First Manifesto

The Dialectics of Love: Part One
(in *Three Young Poets,* edited by Alan Swallow)

To Walk a Crooked Mile

Longshot O'Leary's Garland of Practical Poesy

A Witness to the Times

Figures from a Double World

The Movie at the End of the World
(England; in preparation)

New and Selected Poems

LETTER
to an
IMAGINARY
FRIEND Parts I and II

THOMAS McGRATH

THE SWALLOW PRESS INC.

CHICAGO

Published by
The Swallow Press, Inc.
1139 S. Wabash Avenue
Chicago, Illinois, 60605

LIBRARY OF CONGRESS CATALOG CARD NUMBER 77-81967

Passages from this poem have appeared in *Coastlines* and *American Dialog;* one section appeared in my *New and Selected Poems;* and, thanks to George Hitchcock, a large part of the second book was printed occasionally in his magazine *Kayak*.

I wish to thank Mary Clarke and Glenda Sullivan for help with the ms of the first book. A good deal of the writing of the second book was done while I was on the Amy Lowell Travelling Poetry Scholarship and the ms was completed as part of a year of work made possible for me while I was on a Guggenheim Fellowship.

For Eugenia,
Tomasito,
Che
and the Commune

A NOTE ON THE BOOK

The poem which follows is Book I of a work made up of several books—at least so it seems to me now. But Book I, and each of the two Parts in it, is complete in itself, having a beginning, middle and end etc. etc. as Aristotle, Caudwell and good sense require. The whole poem, when completed, will probably bear the present title: *Letter to an Imaginary Friend*.

The form of Part One of the poem is, if you will, that of pseudo-autobiography—the characters are structures of my own perceptions and feelings. The quotations are for the most part direct speech of people now dead; or they may be speech transposed into my own terms; or they may be, in a few instances, from recognizable literary sources. Occasionally I have paraphrased a line of a poem, or parodied it, or borrowed the rhythm of a line or cadence thinking to establish a second or third grid through which an area of experience may be viewed. And on a couple of occasions, where my own invention seemed inadequate, I have followed the examples of Butch Cassidy and T. S. Eliot, turned bandit, and stolen outright.

The form of Part Two is the same as that of Part One except that it is concerned with the offering of evidences for a revolutionary miracle and with elaborating a ceremony out of these materials to bring such a miracle to pass.

For those interested in such things, perhaps I should say that I think of the metrical base of this poem as being the six beat line. This is not, obviously, true of some of the sections; and even where it *is* true it is not always apparent, since I have sometimes broken the line or cut it in half for what seemed to me the greater value of emphasis. In the last analysis I was more interested in the cadence than the line, but as the poem progresses the autonomy of the line becomes more assured—as I think it should be for the general welfare of American verse.

THOMAS McGRATH

PART ONE

Whenever I see my Friend I speak to him; but the expecter, the man with the ears, is not he. They will complain that you are too hard. O ye that would have the cocoanut wrong side outwards, when next I weep I will let you know.

Thoreau

In the moonlight,
The shadow of the bamboo
Is sweeping the great stairs;
But the dust is not stirred.

Senzaki

I

1.

—"From here it is necessary to ship all bodies east."
I am in Los Angeles, at 2714 Marsh Street,
Writing, rolling east with the earth, drifting toward Scorpio,
                                                    thinking,
Hoping toward laughter and indifference.
"They came through the passes,
                    they crossed the dark mountains in a month of snow,
Finding the plain, the bitter water,
                                the iron rivers of the black North.
Horsemen,
Hunters of the hornless deer in the high plateaus of that country,
They travelled the cold year, died in the stone desert."

Aye, long ago. A long journey ago,
Most of it lost in the dark, in a ruck of tourists,
In the night of the compass, companioned by tame wolves, plagued
By theories, flies, visions, by the anthropophagi . . .

I do not know what end that journey was toward.
—But I am its end. I am where I have been and where
I am going. The journeying destination—at least that . . .
But far from the laughter.
                                        So. Writing:

"The melt of the pig pointed to early spring.
The tossed bones augered an easy crossing.
North, said the mossy fur of the high pines.
West, said the colored stone at the sulphur pool."

2.

—And at the age of five ran away from home.
 (I have never been back. Never left.) I was going perhaps
Toward the woods, toward a sound of water—called by what bird?
Leaving the ark-tight farm in its blue and mortgaged weather

To sail the want-all seas of my five dead summers
Past the dark ammonia-and-horse-piss smelling barn
And the barnyard dust, adrift in the turkey wind
Or pocked with the guniea-print and staggering script
Of the drunken-sailor ducks, a secret language; leaving
Also my skippering Irish father, land-locked Sinbad,
With his head in a song-bag and his feet stuck solid
On the quack-grass-roofed and rusting poop-deck of the north forty,
In the alien corn: the feathery, bearded, and all-fathering wheat.

Leaving my mother, too, with her kindness and cookies,
The whispering, ginghamy, prayers—impossible pigeons—
Whickering into the camphor-and-cookie-crumb dark toward
God in the clothes closet.
                              Damp comforts.
                                                    Tears
Harder than nails.
A mint of loving laughter.

How could I leave them?
I took them with me, though I went alone
Into the Christmas dark of the woods and down
The whistling slope of the coulee, past the Indian graves
Alive and flickering with the gopher light.

                              3.
—Dry runs and practice journeys through the earthquake weather
Of the interior summer . . .
                                        the singing services
And ceremony cheerful as a harness bell.
—Bright flags and fictions of those hyacinthine hours
Stain and sustain me past the hell of this mumming time
Toward the high wake I would hold:
                                        No ghost, but O ill and older
Than other autumns when I ran the calico lanes
Past sleepy summer, gone, and the late west light
Downfallen. Lost. Autumn of distant voices, half heard,
Calling.
                    Rain. Gunfire. Crows. Mist, far, woods.

2

Farther than winter birds in the most gaunt tree
Snapped in the frost, I was; or went. Was free, and haunted
By the reeling plunge of the high hawk down—down! O down
Where the curving rabbit lunged and was slapped with a sharp and killing
Heel.
There, in the still post-solstice dark, among
Rococco snow, the harp-shaped drifts and the ghost-marked trees of the season
I went all ways . . .
—Spring came; the first cold rainstorms, dropping
Their electric hardware in the bright-work of the snow.
Then, the leather seasons by, and my bundling times,
My eye sustained the cow-bird and the crow,
Their feather terms . . .
                    Then horny Summer come . . .
                              —And Autumn growing
In the west steep wrestling light and the rain-wrung rheumy wind in the rag-headed woods . . .

                    *   *   *   *   *   *

Way-stations on the underground journey; the boy running, running . . .
—Search for Lough Derg, or the holy waters of the Cheyenne,
Or the calf-deep Maple. Running away
I had the pleasure of their company . . .

                              4.

Took them? They came—
Past the Horn, Cape Wrath, Oxford and Fifth and Main
Laughing and mourning, snug in the two seater buggy,
Jouncing and bouncing on the gumbo roads
Or slogging loblolly in the bottom lands—
My seven tongued family.
How could I escape? Strapped on the truckle bars
Of the bucking red-ball freights or riding the blinds cold
Or sick and sea-sawed on the seven seas
Or in metal and altitude, drilling the high blue
I fled.
I heard them laughing at the oarsmen's bench.
Conched in cowcatchers, they rambled at my side.
The seat of the buggy was wider than Texas

And slung to the axles were my rowdy cousins;
Riding the whippletrees: aunts, uncles, brothers,
Second cousins, great aunts, friends and neighbors
All holus-bolus, piss-proud, all sugar-and-shit
A goddamned gallimaufry of ancestors.
The high passes?
Hunter of the hornless deer?

5.

A flickering of gopher light. The Indian graves . . .
And then the river.

        Companioned, and alone,
Five, ten, or twenty, I followed the coulee hills
Into the dreaming green of the river shade,
The fish-stinking cow-dunged dark of the cattle-crossing,
The fox-barking, timber-wolf country, where . . .
The cicada was sawing down the afternoon:
Upstream a beaver was spanking Nature:
The cows were wilder:
Horses carniverous.

The kittycorner river cut through the buggy
Through Dachau and Thaelmann
Rolfe in Spain
Through the placid, woodchuck-coughing afternoon
Drifting
Past Greenwich, Baton Rouge, Sheldon, Rome
And past Red Hook and Mobile where the rivers mourn
Old Thames, Missouri, Rio Hondo. Now
In far Los Angeles I hear
The Flying Dutchman in the dry river
Mourning. Mourning.
Ancestral night . . . .

       · · · ·

Passages of the dark; streets with no known turning
Beyond the sleepy midnight and the metaphysical summer
Leading here. Here. Here, queerly here.

To the east slant light of the underground moon, and the rusty garden
Empty.
                    Bounded by ghosts.
                              Empty execpt for footnotes
Of journeying far friends near.

                                        Enter now,
O bird on the green branch of the dying tree, singing
Sing me toward home:
Toward the deep past and inalienable loss:
Toward the gone stranger carrying my name
In the possible future
                              —enter now:
Purlieus and stamping grounds of the hungering people
O enter

"They died in the stone desert
They crossed the dark mountain in the month of snow.
Finding the plain, the bitter water, the iron rivers of the black North."
Horns on the freeway. Footsteps of strangers,
Angelinos: visitations in the metropolitan night.

"Hunters of the hornless deer."

Ancestral baggage . . . .

II

1.

Great God Almighty, but the troubles of the stinking street!
First neighbor on strike since Come Monday, and Second
Neighbor on strike Come Tuesday.

                                   Eggs are dearer,

Bread has entered Marsh Street's realm of value,
And shuffling past Salsipuede Avenue
The age of education comes round the corner . . .

     I was born under an evil star in the black cloud of Lusath,
     Under the early sign of apocalyptic fire . . .
     I live in the distant present, endless indomitable potlatch
     Of journeying
                     far
                             hungering
     Ghosts;
     Amidst collapsing empires of irreversible
     Talk . . . Second Kingdoms and Ming Dynasties of ad hoc
     Exempla: kinked-up argument, a-temporal colloquies armed and dreamy,
     Unstable and wild as confederations of Sioux . . .

2.

And I hear the pad of feet to the union hall—
But that is New York (17th Street) : Showboat Quinn
Goes by barefoot: fanfare of baseball bats—
They are whacking the seamen like mamba gourds down Hudson.
And elsewhere old Mister Peets is saying "Eeyah! He's the man!"—
Listening to Morrison blasting dead Huey Long
As the moon spins over Baton Rouge in the freezing Christmas,
And the waterworks crackle.

                               Plumber Peets cocks an eye,

As the pipes burst like shrapnel and the citizens, crazed,
Unshaven, their bladders bursting, bray at the moon.

At the moon and Peets, who sits at the radio, high
As a coon in a tree, near the rasping gas-fire, sucking
His sugar-tit pipe and his politics.

                                  The Phony War
Sings in the streets.

                     Jimmy plays football.

                                  Warren,
Pinched and poor-favored as a parson's luck,
Carrying his future—that North Sea grave—like a mile
Of invisible water, comes by . . .

    Now, down in these flats, the imagined city dreams
    In its fiery cages . . .
                Cacodemons and Agathodemons
                            struggling in the pit,
    And, in the heavens, the endless feuds and follies of the blazing far stars:
Ancestral vendettas.
                    Among whom I was born,
    Among the flat fields, flat stores, and the bombed-flat burning towns
Under the sign of our degenerate fire . . .

Christ! but it's cold.
My garden bears in its tide the wreckage of summer flowers.
In the south Forty the flax is flat with the rust . . .

                                3.
The bare feet pad in the street.

                         "Eayah!" says the plumber,
"Them cotton-pickin', possum-eatin', mammy-jammers *got* to go!"
His ear is cocked, while half of Baton Rouge
Pisses in the freezing street.
                          Peets is toasting his pinkies
Sending his nine-foot wife for a jug of gin,
Listening.
                Will He win? Will O. K. Allen, will
Morrison win?
                      Anarcho-solipsist contraventions . . .
Under the hysteria of the tide-containing moon
The burghers rage. (They are hanging fresh sides of beef

in the frost-bound dashas of their morning-rooms,
Dahvening to Peets) . . .
And Quinn goes by in the street (Seventeenth) and my neighbors
Are striking on Marsh in that future where Warren is dead
And my brother dead . . .

      The flowers rust in my garden, pointing
      Toward farthest Autumn.
                            The flax is flat
    In the freezing heat.

And the plumber
("The folded arms of the workers," says Warren)
Pulls at his aural tether . . .

4.

Out of imperfect confusion, to argue a purer chaos . . .
I've lived, truly, in a Custer's Massacre of sad sacks
Who sang in my ear their histories and my own.
And out of these ghosts I bring these harvest dead
Into the light of speech . . .
Where now the citizens dream in a sleep of fire—
No more than a mountain breath, pulse-beat of rock—
Toward this distant present, in this nightjourney where all—

Borne beyond Libra
Southward
Borne toward the Gulf, the whole shooting-match of these times
In the hiss and jostle of the Mississippi
The living and the dead
To the revolving graves and the glass pastures of the fined-down diamond-cutting Sea.

III

1.

Out of the whirring lamp-hung dusk my mother calls.
From the lank pastures of my sleep I turn and climb,
From the leathery dark where the bats work, from the coasting
High all-winter all-weather christmas hills of my sleep.
And there is my grandfather chewing his goatee,
Prancing about like a horse. And the drone and whir from
     the fields
Where the thresher mourns and showers on the morning stillness
A bright fistful of whistles.

The water-monkey is late, the straw-monkey
Is late and the bundle-stiffs are late and my grandfather dances
In the yellowy kerosene smell of the morning lamps where my mother
Brightens a dish on her apron and feeds the stove
Its iron, round crackling mouth and throat full of bristling flame,
Gold in the five o'clock morning night.
Dances and raves. A worker has broken his wrist;
The machine is whistling its brass-tongued rage and the jack- booted weathers of autumn
Hiss and sing in the North.
The rains are coming, and the end of the world
Is coming.
         My grandfather dances.
I am slowly fed into my B.V.D.'s while the still-dark day
Assumes the structure of my nine year world,
And the whistle hoots.

"You'll be the straw-monkey. Can ye do it boy?"
My grandfather capers about while I assemble my parts
And my mother fusses. Is the job too hard?
"Ach, woman, the chiselur's tall as a weed!
He's not to be spike-pitchin', a whistle-punk only—
Sure it's a breeze of a job and he'll sit in the shade on his bum
The day long."
    She pets me and cooks:
Bacon and eggs and the bitter, denatured coffee

Of man's estate. While my grandfather stamps and grumbles
And my brothers tumble from sleep into the kitchen,
Questioning. Owl-eyed and envious.

A kiss and a hug. A piece of pie in my pocket
For love and luck.

                         Then, in a jingle of trace chains,
The martingale's chatter and squeak of straps in their keepers,
I drove the big roan team through the grey of the chill morning,
My mother waving.
                 Goodby
And the kids staring, still sleepy,
Myself proud and scared and the echo of sleep still strong
In my veins. (The reins I'd looped round my hips so the fast-stepping team
Half pulled me, stiff legged, and tacking about like a boat
In their dusty wake) .
                     Ahead my grandfather's buggy
Bounced down the coulee hill, up the opposite slope
Toward the threshing machine and its whistling brass commandments,
The barb-tongued golden barley and the tents of the biblical wheat,
Frontiers of sweat and legendary field
Of manhood.

Behind me my mother called.   Something I could not hear.
The kids stood solemn
                  Still in the weather of childhood.
Waved.
        Throwing kisses.
                Waved my hand in return.
So long.
So long.
So long.

2.

Blind. Out of the labyrinthine sleep
Of childhood I entered the brilliant alien arena
Blind in the harsh light.

                              Entered too soon, too young,
Bobbing along on the lines, dragged by a team of roans,
 (Whose names *should* have been Poverty and Pride)
Into the world of men at the age of nine

This was no ritual visit; no summer foray,
Scouting party or cook-out in the Big Horn country
With the ridge-pole pine singing my honor and the streams full of fish and fancy,
The light-fall valorous and God-creatures taller than tales
To teach me camp-craft, to put a crimp in the nightmare,
To fan my six gun.
Oh, I know that ten-sleep camp where the ticking Dechard rifle
Dozes by the banker's son, the half-real shooting gallery
Of the Dream Range where red-skin and deer ride by
On an endless belt and the bear pop up, pop down,
In front of the painted scene of lake and mountain,
Where prizes are always given . . .
                              Aloft on the shaking deck,
Half blind and deafened in the roaring dust,
On the heaving back of the thresher,
My neck blistered by sun and the flying chaff, my clothes
Shot full of thistles and beards, a gospel itch,
Like a small St. Stephen, I turned the wheel of the blower
Loading the straw-rack.
The whistle snapped at my heels: in a keening blizzard
Of sand-burrs, barley-beards and beggars-lice, in a red thunder
Where the wheat rust bellowed up in a stormy cloud
From the knife-flashing feeder,
I turned the wheel.
Far from Tom Swift, and farther
From troop Nine, the cabin they built on the river.

3.
The rites of passage toward the stranger's country,
The secret language foreign as a beard . . .
 I turned in machine-made circles: first from the screaming red
 Weather where the straw stack grew and the rattling thresher mourned;

13

Then to the rocking engine where the fly-wheel flashed and labored
And the drive-belt waxed and waned, the splices clapped at its cross
Ebbing and flowing, slack or taut as the spikers
Dropped the bivouaced wheat in the feeder's revolving throat.

Feathered in steam like a great tormented beast
The engine roared and laughed, dreamed and complained,
And the pet-cocks dripped and sizzled; and under its fiery gut
Stalactites formed from the hand-hold's rheumy slobbers.
—Mane of sparks, metallic spike of its voice,
The mile-long bacony crackle of burning grease!
There the engineer sat, on the high drivers,
Aloof as a God. Filthy. A hunk of waste
Clutched in one gauntleted hand, in the other the oil can
Beaked and long-necked as some exotic bird;
Wreathed in smoke, in the clatter of loose eccentrics.
And the water-monkey, back from the green quiet of the river
With a full tank, was rolling a brown quirrly
(A high school boy) hunkered in the dripping shade
Of the water-tender, in the tall talk and acrid sweat
Of the circle of spitting stiffs whose cloud-topped bundle-racks
Waited their turns at the feeder.
And the fireman: goggled, shirtless, a flashing-three tined fork,
Its handle charred, stuck through the shiny metallic
Lip of the engine, into the flaming, smoky
Fire-box of its heart.
Myself: straw-monkey. Jester at court.

So, dawn to dusk, dark to dark, hurried
From the booming furious brume of the thresher's back
To the antipodean panting engine. Caught in the first
Circle.

Was it hard? I don't know. It was terrifying.
The whistle snapped and I ran. The thresher moaned on its glut.
The Danaean rain of the wheat rained down.
Hard? No. Everyone wanted to help me.
My father, riding the grain-tanks from the field

To the town elevators, starting out in the chilly dawn
And home at the cold midnight, eating when time allowed,
Doing the work of a threshing hand and the chores of the farm
                    to boot,
Harnessing the team I was too short to harness,
Helping me pick up a load when he got back from town
In the jolting musical empty grain tank.
                                        He had boils that summer,
His neck was circled with ruby light, I remember.
Poulticed with heated bottles.
My mother helped. I had cookies stuffed in my pocket,
Ginger . . .
Their crumbly sweetness.
                            Worrying:
"Jim, is it too hard?
The boy's tired as a horse."
My grandfather too,
After the first week, when they found a man,
Came prancing and dancing, pulling his thin beard:
"Kate, let the boy be quitting.
It's hard, long hours. Let him quit."
My father came in the dark
 (Where I'd gone into sleep, into the open flaming
Mouth of the dream, the whistle biting my ears,
The night vibrating,
In the fog of the red rust, steam, the rattle of concaves)
Came about midnight.
His last chore done, he led me into the bright
Kitchen. (The table was already set for breakfast;
The potatoes were sliced; the pie, cross cut; a cloth
Fenced out the flies.)
Then, his supper, we ate ice cream and cheese;
Sardines; crackers; tomatoes still wet with the night
Out of the garden; cucumbers crisp and salty
Cooled in the watertrough; bacon and watermelon
Left over from supper.
"Tom, Old Timer," he'd say. "Ain't you had enough?
This workin' won't get you nowheres. Let the job go.

We got a man for her now."
But I couldn't. No way to quit.
My hand was stuck to the plough and I cried to stay.
 (As at morning, with the sleep stuck in my eyes and my morning
                breakfast
Dead in my stomach I cried for the day to be gone) .

I couldn't quit. I came out of sleep at four
Dazed and dreaming and ate my food on the run,
And ran to the barn; the roan team knelt and dozed;
I clapped the harness on them and kicked them awake
And rode the off one, galloping, into the field
Where the engine slept in its heat.
The fireman grunted. He struck a match to his fork.
The crackling fireball, thrust to the metal heart,
Ignited the still dark day.

Sometimes, at night, after a long move to another farm,
Hours after the bundle-teams were gone and sleeping,
After we'd set the rig for the next day,
I rode the off-horse home.
Midnight, maybe, the dogs of the strange farms
Barking behind me, the river short-cut rustling
With its dark and secret life and the deep pools warm.
 (I swam there once in the dead of night while the team
Nuzzled the black water) .
Home then. Dead beat.

To quit was impossible once you had started.
All you could do was somehow to learn the ropes.
No one could teach you.
When you were late the whistle
Blasted you into the kingly estate
Of the daylight man. Responsibility. The hot foundries
Of the will.
                But when, your load up, you squatted
In the spitting circle of stiffs, in the hot shade
Under the sky-piled bundle-racks waiting their turn
                at the feeder,

16

Chewing on rose apples and bumming a smoke—
You were no man there.
A man to the engine's hunger, to the lash of the whistle,
But not to the tough young punks from Detroit or Chicago
Drifting the tide of the harvest the first time
And jealous of manhood.
                                        Not to the old stiffs
Smoke shooters, their bindles weighted with dust
From Kansas to Calgary.
                                        Not to your uncle surely
Boss of the rig who slapped you once when you swore,
Before the ritual was known or the language of men.

O great port of the Dream! Gate to the fearful country,
So near and magically far, what key will open?
Their alien smell, their talk, their foreign hungers,
And something awful, secret: I saw them, lost,
Borne on the fearful stream in a sinful valor
And longed to enter. To know. To burn in that fire.

                             4.
My father took me as far as he could that summer,
Those midnights, mostly, back from his long haul.
But mostly Cal, one of the bundle teamsters,
My sun-blackened Virgil of the spitting circle,
Led me from depth to depth.
                                        Toward the light
I was too young to enter.
He must have been about thirty. As thin as a post,
As tough as whang-leather, with a brick-topped mulish face,
A quiet talker. He read *The Industrial Worker,*
Though I didn't know what the paper was at the time.
The last of the real Wobs—that, too, I didn't know,
Couldn't.
                   Played a harmonica; sat after supper
In the lantern smell and late bat-whickering dusk,
Playing mumbly-peg and talked of wages and hours
At the bunkhouse door. On Sunday cleaned his gun,

A Colt .38 that he let me shoot at a hawk—
It jumped in my hand and my whole arm tingled with shock.
A quiet man with the smell of the road on him,
The smell of far places. Romantic as all of the stiffs
Were romantic to me and my cousins,
Stick-in-the-mud burgesses of boyhood's country.

What he tried to teach me was how to take my time,
Not to be impatient, not to shy at the fences,
Not to push on the reins, not to baulk nor pull leather.
Tried to teach me when to laugh and when to be serious,
When to laugh at the serious, be serious in my laughter,
To laugh at myself and be serious with myself.
He wanted me to grow without growing too fast for myself.
A good teacher, a brother.

5.

That was the year, too, of the labor troubles on the rigs—
The first, or the last maybe. I heard the talk.
It was dull. Then, one day—windy—
We were threshing flax I remember, toward the end of the run—
After quarter-time I think—the slant light falling
Into the blackened stubble that shut like a fan toward the headland—
The strike started then. Why *then* I don't know.
Cal spoke for the men and my uncle cursed him.
I remember that ugly sound, like some animal cry touching me
Deep and cold, and I ran toward them
And the fighting started.
My uncle punched him. I heard the breaking crunch
Of his teeth going and the blood leaped out of his mouth
Over his neck and shirt—I heard their gruntings and strainings
Like love at night or men working hard together,
And heard the meaty thumpings, like beating a grain sack
As my uncle punched his body—I remember the dust
Jumped from his shirt.
He fell in the blackened stubble
Rose
Was smashed in the face
Stumbled up

18

Fell
Rose
Lay on his side in the harsh long slanting sun
And the blood ran out of his mouth and onto his shoulder.

Then I heard the quiet and that I was crying—
They had shut down the engine.
                                        The last of the bundle-teams
Was coming in at a gallop.
                                        Crying and cursing
Yelled at the crew: "Can't you jump the son-of-a-bitch!
Cal! Cal! get up"
But he didn't get up.
None of them moved.
Raging at my uncle I ran.
Got slapped,
Ran sobbing straight to the engine.
I don't know what I intended. To start the thing maybe,
To run her straight down the belt and into the feeder
Like a vast iron bundle.
I jammed the drive-lever over, lashed back on the throttle,
And the drive belt popped and jumped and the thresher groaned,
The beaters clutched at the air, knives flashed,
And I wrestled the clutch.
                                        Far away, I heard them
Yelling my name, but it didn't sound like my own,
And the clutch stuck. (Did I want it to stick?) I hammered it
And the fireman came on a run and grabbed me and held me
Sobbing and screaming and fighting, my hand clenched
On the whistle rope while it screamed down all of our noises—
Stampeding a couple of empties into the field—
A long, long blast, hoarse, with the falling, brazen
Melancholy of engines when the pressure's falling.

Quiet then. My uncle was cursing the Reds,
Ordering the rig to start, but no one started.
The men drifted away.
                                        The water monkey

19

Came in with his load.

                    Questioned.
He got no answer.
Cal's buddy and someone else got him up
On an empty rack and they started out for home,
Him lying on the flat rack-bed.

Still crying, I picked up his hat that lay in the churned up dust,
And left my rack and team and my uncle's threats,
And cut for home across the river quarter.

                    6.
Green permission . . .

                    Dusk of the brass whistle . . .
Gooseberry dark.
Green moonlight of willow.
Ironwood, basswood and the horny elm.
June berry; box-elder; thick in the thorny brake
The black choke cherry, the high broken ash and the slick
White bark of poplar.

                    I called the king of the woods,
The wind-sprung oak.

                    I called the queen of ivy,
Maharani to his rut-barked duchies;
Summoned the foxgrape, the lank woodbine,
And the small flowers: the wood violets, the cold
Spears of the iris, the spikes of the ghostflower—
It was before the alphabet of trees
Or later.

                    Runeless I stood in the green rain
Of the leaves.

          Waiting.

                    Nothing.

                    Echo of distant horns.

Then

Under the hush and whisper of the wood,
I heard the echoes of the little war.

A fox barked in the hills; and a red hawk boomed
Down on the darkening flats in a feathery splash of hunger.
Silence and waiting.
                                    The rivery rustle
Of a hunting mink.
                        Upstream in the chuckling shallows
A beaver spanked the water where, in its time,
The dam would be where my brother, now in his diapers,
Would trap for the beaver's grandsons.

                                              I could not
See in that green dark.
                                    I went downstream
Below the crossing where I'd swum the midnight river
On my way home from a move.
                                    I put my clothes,
Stinking with sweat and dusty (I thought:
How the dust had jumped from Cal's shirt!)
                              I put them on the broken stump.

I dived from the hummock where the cut-bank crumbled.

Under the river the silence was humming, singing:
Night-song.
                              In the arrest and glaucous light
Delicate, snake-like, the water-weed waved and retracted.
The water sang. The blood in my ears whistled.
I roared up out of the river into the last of the sunlight.

Then: I heard the green singing of the leaves;
The water-mystery,
The night-deep and teasing terror on the lone river
Sang in my bones,
And under its eves and seas I broke my weeping,
In that deeper grieving,
The long, halting—the halt and the long hurry—
Toward the heaving, harsh, the green blurring of the salt mysterious sea.

7.

Later, climbing the coulee hills in the sandy dusk,
After sundown in the long northern twilight,

The night hawk circling where the ragamuffin crows
Steered for the cloudy wood;
In that dead calm, in that flat light,
 (The water darkening where the cattle stood to their knees)
I heard the singing of the little clan.
Comfort of crickets and a thrum of frogs.
Sleepy rustle of birds.

In the dusk the bats hustled.
The hawk wheeled and whirled on the tall perch of the air;
Whirled, fell
Down a long cliff of light, sliding from day into dusk.
Something squealed in the brake.
The crickets were silent.
The cattle lifted their blank and unregardant
Gaze to the hills.
Then, up the long slope of air on his stony, unwavering wing
The hawk plunged upward into a shower of light.

The crickets sang. The frogs
Were weaving their tweeds in the river shallows.

Hawk swoop.

                    Silence.
                                        Singing.
The formal calls of a round-dance.
This riddling of the river-mystery I could not read.

Then, climbing the high pass of my loss, I tramped
Up the dark coulee.
                            The farmyard dark was dappled
With yellowy ponds of light, where the lanterns hung.
It was quiet and empty.
                                    In the hot clutter
Of the kitchen my mother was weeping. "He wouldn't eat."
She said, meaning Cal.
                            She had a womanly notion
(Which she didn't really believe) that all man's troubles
Could be ended by eating—it was a gesture she made
To soothe the world.

My father had driven my uncle out of the yard
Because Cal was *our* man, and not to be mistreated
Any more than horses or dogs. He was also my father's friend.
I got some supper and took it out to the barn.
In the lemony pale light of a lantern, at the far end,
He lay in a stall. His partner sat in the straw
Beside him, whittling, not looking at me. I didn't ask
Where his gun was, that slept in an oily rag
In his suitcase.

                                 I put the food beside him
As I'd done with sick dogs.

                                 He was gone where my love
Nor my partisanship could reach him.

Outside the barn my father knelt in the dust
In the lantern light, fixing a harness. Wanting
Just to be around, I suppose, to try to show Cal
He couldn't desert him.

                             He held the tubular punch
With its spur-like rowle, punching a worn hame strap
And shook the bright copper rivets out of a box.
"Hard lines, Tom," he said. "Hard lines, Old Timer."
I sat in the lantern's circle, the world of men,
And heard Cal breathe in his stall.

                             An army of crickets
Rasped in my ear.

                        "Don't hate anybody."
My father said.
I went toward the house through the dark.

That night the men all left.

                          Along toward morning
I heard the rattle of Fords. They had left Cal there
In the bloody dust that day but they wouldn't work after that.
"The folded arms of the workers" I heard Warren saying,
Sometime in the future where Mister Peets lies dreaming
Of a universal voting-machine.

                          And Showboat
Quinn goes by (New York, later) "The fuckin' proletariat

Is in love with its fuckin' chains. How do you put this fuckin'
Strike on a cost-plus basis?"

There were strikes on other rigs that day, most of them lost,
And, on the second night, a few barns burned.
After that a scattering of flat alky bottles,
Gasoline filled, were found, buried in bundles.

"The folded arms of the workers."
I see Sodaberg
Organizing the tow boats.
                                        I see him on Brooklyn Bridge,
The fizzing dynamite fuse as it drops on the barges.
Then Mac with his mournful face comes round the corner
 (New York) up from the blazing waterfront, preaching
His strikes.
                    And my neighbors are striking on Marsh Street.
(L.A., and later)
                                        And the hawk falls.

A dream-borne singing troubles my still boy's sleep
In the high night where Cal had gone:
                                        They came through
The high passes, they crossed the dark mountains
In a month of snow.
Finding the plain, the bitter water, the iron
Rivers of the black north . . .

Hunters
                    in the high plateaus of that country . . .

Climbing toward sleep . . .

But far
                    from the laughter.

IV

1.

The immortal girls, the summer manifestoes,
Startle the buzzard in the corpse-bearing tree.

Explosion of daisies in the stricken field.
The lilac is lifting its lavender toward Arcturus.

Noon's incandescence, autonomy of night,
Cracked open throttles on my resurrection bone,
My moon-steered master, midnight fisherman,
Bound for the Indies . . .

Coiffeur of dream, oh bright improbable gold!
The blonde haired women, crowned as with surplus light,
Curls crisp as lettuce on their bellies porch
And slick and secret when the armpit yawns—
Hair! dimension of heat!
                              Lit by subliminal suns
That shrink their dresses half way up their thighs
It ripens outward.
                              Furry as a peach
It licks the hand that hungers at the knee;
And where the back and buttocks sweetly mate
Like queenly empires joined in natural peace
(Equation of the palm! O sweet division!)
Glints like shot silk. And where the pubis thrusts
Into my world to light me into dark
Is stiff and secret as a buried fence
Or bristles friendly as a welcome mat.

Yes: and those soft brunettes, their eyes like caves
Their third eye winking in the knowing dark!
O ox-eyed honeys with the wine dark hair,
Branches of midnight where all moon long I crowed,
Punching our tickets on the train toward dawn—
How black your hair!

                                        Belly of smoky wheat,
Alabastrine buttocks, legs like a slow dream—
Oh as to a citizen of Jupiter's moons,
Your soft enormous breasts, over the bare horizon,
Loom, golden and dusky rose, tremendous planets
Pendulous . . .
Iris toward the nipple and the nipples pink, veiny
Shot with faint blue . . .
And your eyes, O magnificent black haired women!
Invincibly glazed or wet as a pool-side stone,
Heavy with sleep; and your mouths wide and elastic,
And your lips, thickened with heat, which your tongue keeps wetting!
Ah, woman with your ass as thick as a pillow,
With your thighs like deadfalls and the black nest of your sex
Like a midnight hungry quicksand where I drown!
Drown and am born. Upborne! Resurrected!
Startling the buzzard on my shoulder tree!
I've come through your black pass many's the sunny night!

And the brown haired women, slim, with their lenten graces,
Or short and thickset and busy as a bear,
Their knees dimpled and their hips slung like a hammock,
Their bellies snug to my gut as a flesh muff;
And the red-heads, electric, with their buttermilk skin
And the tickle inside the knee, and their burning bush,
With its wise unsleeping bird, more dark than their eyebrows—
Bucking like goats, quicker than minks, randy
As the wild strawberry roan: sunfishing by moonlight
They have ridden me into a stall where I sleep standing up.

                                2.
Sweet Jesus at morning the queenly women of our youth!
The monumental creatures of our summer lust!
Sweet fantastic darlings, as full of juice as plums,
Pneumatic and backless as a functional dream
Where are ye now?
Where were ye then, indeed?

                        26

Walking three-legged in the sexual haze,
Drifting toward the Lion on the bosomy hills of summer,
In the hunting light, the marmareal bulge of the moon,
I wooed them barebacked in the saddling heat.

First was Inez, her face a looney fiction,
Her bottom like concrete and her wrestling arms;
Fay with breasts as hard as hand grenades
(Whose father's shot gun dozed behind the door),
Barefooted Rose, found in the bottom lands
(We layed the flax as flat as forty horses,
The blue bells showering); Amy with her long hair
Drawn in mock modesty between long legs;
And Sandy with her car, who would be driving and do it;
And June who would roll you as in a barrel down hill—
The Gaelic torture; Gin with her snapping trap,
The heliotropic quim: locked in till daybreak;
Literary Esther, who could fox your copy,
And the double Gladys, one blonde, one black.

O great kingdom of Fuck! And myself: plenipotentiary!
Under the dog star's blaze, in the high rooms of the moonlight,
In the doze and balance of the wide noon,
I hung my pennant from the top of the windy mast:
Jolly Roger sailing the want-not seas of the summers.
And under the coupling of the wheeling night
Muffled in flesh and clamped to the sweaty pelt
Of Blanche or Betty, threshing the green baroque
Stacks of the long hay—the burrs stuck in our crotch,
The dust thick in our throats so we sneezed in spasm—
Or flat on the floor, or the back seat of a car,
Or a groaning trestle table in the Methodist Church basement,
And far in the fields, and high in the hills, and hot
And quick in the roaring cars: by the bridge, by the river,
In Troop Nine's dank log cabin where the Cheyenne flows:
By light, by dark, up on the roof, in the celler,
In the rattling belfry where the bats complained,
Or backed against trees, or against the squealing fences,

Or belly to belly with no place to lie down
In the light of the dreaming moon.

3.

Dog watch and silence.
                    In the high school yard, the dust
Settles; of vanished cars, the vast nocturnal migrations.
Under the moon,
Paler than flowers the condoms gleam on the lawn.
Delicate, blue,
Fragrance of lilacs drifts in the night air, purer,
Sweeter than moonlight.

The lilac points to Arcturus.
Points down the street to my Grandfather's clapboard house,
To the gimcrack moldering porch where a beehive sleeps in the wall,
Toward his Irish keening.
"Ay-you, Tom. Avoid the occasion of sin.
You're a quick hand with a book. Pick up an education
And don't run around be the night!
                              Boy, it's a wide
Road runs down to hell and its clear coasting
And the skids are greased for the poor. Boy, be learning!"
And up to bed, past the squeaking third step, bearing
Through the whispering grandfather dust, in the bellowing night of my sex
My little learning (Gladys and Daisy) bearing
The golden apple of my discontent.

4.

The dust settles. Settles like time, The years
Swing round my head like birds. It is fall, now, evening,
The long and lonesome season.
The car bumps on the wagon road. In the lights
The dust is thick. The cattle hump and shuffle.
The smell of the Autumn river in the cold night air
Is wild and alien.

Out of the river pasture,
Out of the gone summer we drive the cattle.
They plod the road, blind in the carlight's dazzle,
Docile enough. The car bumps and complains.
Wally is driving. The car crawls in low gear
And the dash light gleams in the hair of my littlest brother.
"Where will you go?" he says. "Is it far to the town
Where they keep the college?"
                              He is five years old, maybe seven.
"What will you learn to know?"

I know it is warm in the car. The night stiffens
With black frost but the car is warm. What shall we learn
In the cold? In the cold country where the books are burning?
Across the classroom of the north forty
My father professes his love and labor.
In the black field, burnt now, where the flax'
Small breakers ran, the Wobblies' footprint is buried.
A cold moon hangs in the trees.

"I hate September," says Wally. "The damn blank lonesome fields—
What will you learn anyway?"
And Jack says, sleepy, leaning his furry head
Into my side:
"Is it far? Is it long?"

                              5.

And returned then, up the coulee hills from the river
Later than gopher light, with the colder and older moon
Riding my back like a buzzard.
                              Past the squeaking third
Step on the granfather stair, past the dusty
Belfry and Daisy caught in the lilac,
Past barns where the country wenches were singing like cardinal sins—
And do they sing in the dust still?
                              Do their bones
Sing in the golden dust in the stallion summers?

29

O small girls with your wide knowledge, you led me
Into the continent of guilt and forgiving, where love is;
Through the small gate of your sex I go into my kingdom.
Teachers of men! O hot, great hearted women
The world turns still on the axis of your thighs!

V

1.

Love and hunger!—that is my whole story.
An education in the form of a night journey
Congo of the heart . . .
                            Dream voyage . . .
                                                        Safari
To the dark interior.
Chaffinch, miner's canary, O white mice
Of Sir Humphrey Davy be with me now!

Borne on the underground stream,
I entered the hornacle mine—trivium—quadrivium—
In the rattling Ford, through the black stopes of a dust storm
From Sheldon to Buffalo.
                                    Stopped in that dead of night,
The midnight noon of nineteen-thirty-five,
Becalmed in a dark our headlights could not pierce
And my father gave me advice. Advice and ten dollars
The money to last for a year, the advice for a lifetime.
I heard the wind howl in the night of the dust:
Somewhere a freight was poking a snout of sound
Through all that flying real estate.
And through the dark and the future I hear Showboat Quinn:
"What part in the fuckin' pageant of history did *you* play?"
Far horns.
The iron breath of the train.
A little treasury of Montana sifts in at the window.

What was he saying? What was my father saying?
He was wishing me luck, he was saying love in a language
That has no word for it, the language of fathers and sons.
He was saying that school would be hard, that times were
Hard, and that life was hard.
                            Country news.
                                                    History

Blown past your headlights.

And the clanking box cars banged on over the dead men,
Bearing the dead Communist—but that is all in the future—
And Cal is riding a reefer lined with the ice
Of an earlier summer.

                        Borne east-south-east as the night
Shakes all around me . . .

                                Toward the high passes.
When the storm had lifted enough to see we went on.

2.

How now, Poor Richard, with that ten dollar pie in your pocket,
In your cousin's fur-collared coat like a moulting scarecrow!

Under the sign of Virgo I came to State College.
At Fargo, North Dakota, where the Red River flows north,
A far country.

                        "Where fatherhood was not honored,
Conception being attributed to the North
Wind, or the eating of beans, or the accidental
Swallowing of an insect."

                              Still they did not believe
That "snakes were incarnations of the dead"
Cast the bones of sheep for signs of the weather
Paint still lives of the interiors of horses—
A most sensible people.
So come there with my scholarship and the notion
Of learning.
And the first man I met was some kind of dean.
O excellent title!
What did it mean? Did the tumbleweed
Blowing out of Saskatchewan know it?
A man, anyhow, thin as a rail and mean
As a cross-barred barb-wire gate, with flat face to him
Like Picasso's Vallauris plates; all piss and moment,
A pithy, pursy bastard, like a quidnunc espaliered
Against the ass of the North Wind.

He sat there like a chilly Lutheran Buddha,
All two dimensions of him—you could hear the storm
Boom up through his splined backside with a sound like a jug-blowers ceilidh.
Sat there and said that to go to his college
I must stay in such-and-such dorm, designed for Freshmen,
Built by himself and some other learned doctors
And later to be presented to the college itself
When it was paid for.

                              And when he and his golden twins
Had been well paid for.

                              But I couldn't swing it,
Having no money to live like a proper student.

And sat there. Nestled on the cold col of his nose
 (His astral hand, involved in taking the damper
Was caught in a till that was still five years in the future)
His pince nez, gemini of radar, tracking
Invisible flies, rode through a zodiac
Numbering all signs but my own.

Well, that is how it goes.

                              The bastard sat there
Like a man with a paper ass-hole, like a man
With his head under water, talking talking.

                              At last his words

Said nothing but *money money*. A conversation
We could not enter.
"Somebody should set fire to the son of a bitch."
I hear Mac saying.

                              Seventeenth Street is jammed
With flags and seamen. May Day, '46.
"Somebody should tamp up on the hyperboreon bugger!"
And my father says "The dirty muzzler!"

                              And the flags toss
As we go out in a storm that's ten years strong,
Where the freight cars rattle and the vigorous dead of the future
Ride in the reefers, preserved in invisible ice.
Dakota, Montana

                              Blowing along on the wind

33

Those dusty slogans

                                                                    Alive.

                              3.
God damn it to hell, the cargo a man has to carry
And all the streets in the moon as slick as glass!

That's how I went to the country of the Swedes, Minnesota,
To school there, in a college over in Moorhead.
A no-story structure of purest dream, a hornacle mine
Rampant.
                    By night those brick-built blondes
Turned up their pretty tails to scholastic gentry
That would be dreaming of their seminars
Through the cold classes where they learned to teach.

To teach by Christ! They hadn't learned to read,
To write, to think, to wipe their asses properly—
To teach!

                                        And I was to learn to teach
Like it or not.

                                    Thinking I wanted to learn
To think, I didn't like it.

                                        So, was taught
To teach by teachers who could neither think nor teach—
Taught harum-scarum and arsy-varsy to teach!
Oh, they will teach you to worship Pallas Athena,
Those education departments!

                                    Anything unsexed
Sprung out of an empty head . . .

                                    Anyway, that's how it was
A surrogate college.

                                    Still I spent my time
In the library—a quack-grass and sow-thistle
Patch of books in a warm building with windows
Looking out on that same pageant of history

That Showboat Quinn contemned.

                              Perhaps I learned how to teach
Five minutes one day when my mind was wandering—
I grew to a teacher, later.

                              Meantime, I read.
I walked five miles to the college and then walked back
And lunched at noon on a five-cent bar of candy
They don't make any more.
                    Ambrosia.
                              Proust.
Troubled by sleep, my tiger-lined room.
                              And Eliot
(What will the young take for guides in their chilly country!)
Was with me as I crossed the river, on my way to school,
Where the unemployed fished, the fish badly out-numbered,
At morning.
                    At evening as I came home,
The ravenous poor were doing side-leaps from hunger
At the river where one old gar was shaking the water with fright.
By then the winter rains had come. The streets were glassy,
With ice. With their grey beards stiff in the angry wind,
Belly down on the burnished avenues,
The burgers sledded south like homing geese.

O season of the horizontal! The Marat,
The Anacharsis Cloots of the five seasons!
Anagogic leveller, commune of mystical ice!
Hallelujah! Everything dead on the level
For once!
                    In the didder and horripilation
Of mind and matter, the pants of the long blondes
Come down, the post office was raided and the post-master general
Was found to be short ninety-million dead letters
In each of which was a gopher tail, and an ad
From Hercules Sandow, the prime god of that country,
And a splinter of the True Cross.

All for the American Dream!
The banks collapsed, the depositors
Were folded away like flowers in the night's cold book—
In a smell of tamped dynamite, in the light of the penny
Sales where the farmers, shotguns in their hands,
Were buying back land the Ogalalla Sioux
Had scalped them for!

In those days, in the icy galleries of noon,
When the belly-down poor, their noses flat on the roof
Of the stiffened river glared at the solitary gar;
When the mayor, taking his stand, walked all one day
Crossing the frictionless intersection of Hope and Truth:
Failed to arrive; when the journeying city fathers,
Flat on their navels as migratory fish
But howling their despair like banshees, slid down the
                                        amethyst street
Toward Wahpeton, and southward—
Oh, all was equal then!
Like cattle caught in a storm our sterns to the pole star
We humped for warmth together.
                              In those days, in the snow
In the fiery cold of the library's brumal arettes—
The boreal light of the public and published dark—
Climbing like Tenzing, I found, in the frost-furred bright
Kitchens and cirques (among the petrified bats
And stuffed condoms—all of the Second Empire)
And in the ice ranches of the maverick intellect
Deep underground—down there, I say,
Among man-eating horses and the antipodean bears
Who wear their assholes preludant like the open eye
Of a Dechard rifle (in the blind-storm, in the thick
Of the mine-gas—and me with that damn dead bird,
Chaffinch, canary, or a white mouse maybe, stuck in my pocket
Where I'd hoped to find a chocolate bar)
                                        —O there
All odds were even.
                    The lion and the lamb

Lay down, sideways. Collapsed.

                                        Fox and Wolfe

Supported each other. A book on dreams
Buttressed the *Crisis in Physics*. And Marx and Bakunin
At last at peace. It was the cold did it—
It stopped their peristalsis near the left ventricle of the moon.

                              4.

Circularity! That's half the curse of the times:
It is to stop the circulation of circulating
Libraries—that's the trouble. I did.
Put everything down as flat as the skating fathers
Going by on their beards.

                              That spare silhouette
Is hard to get a bead on: a low elevation—
It's enough to make you look twice at the face of the dead.
There's the equality of the Five Mile Shelf:
And everyone equal.

To shake like a dog in the cold
Is not so bad when everyone else must do it—
That's civilization prime, a bearable thing.
But to dodge cadillacs when your knees are cut off at your elbows ...
No. Put the books out, all flat on the table,
Like the break-up of the Yukon—let the bloodhounds bay,
Little Eliza will cross on the ice flow, her tail one snap
Ahead of their judgment.
Cold winter, then! Maximum entropy
End of circularity, everyone flat in the streets,
Equal.

                              That's when I saw for the first time
Iron-jawed George, Jefferson with his flutes and farms
And radical Madison—all of them deader than mackerel.
Those dead don't budge.
No, in that polar light, all directions are North,
You must choose your stars there.

5.

So: I found my directions: by the blue moss
On the north side of a book, by the colored stone
In the eye of a blind professor, and steered ahead.

In the horizontal night, with everyone flat on his face
Pushed by the tides of the moon, sliding toward third
In the sempiternal anguish of suburban streets
Order! Sweet order!

                      In the busy leather of the old archives
Professor G. is weighing up the proof
That Bakunin wrote Marx.

                        South of the black ice
Where I crossed the river near the fishing poor
Toward the falls

         Open water

              The fish are eating the unemployed.

"An education now," Peets says. "Eeyah
It puts your mind in a practical order."
"Piss in your hand an' it gets wet," says Peets.
Order!
       Order everywhere!
South on the ice, belly down, the citizens tighten formation.
A man, standing up on his hind feet can see for miles . . .
No one else standing to break his view.
Order! Order!

How cold it is!

The blue eye of the moon is stuck full of bones.

VI

1.

Home, then, where the loss is: the rusty ports of the sun.

December's dog days, when the stalk of the gospel Light
Leans out of winter weaker than the moon—
They sang me home.

                                  I came then, I remember,
In the down-hill rattle of the ransomed Ford with the hustling wind
Filing the night time quiet and the dull scar of the road
With a white gentry of mixed sand and snow . . .
Past the night-shut dreaming farms, fixed in the bright enamel
Of the full-filled sentry moon.

                                  In the high piled, tight
Barns, the crystalline, white beards of the frost were growing—
Fierce acres of gone summer, now stunned in the shut-knife cold
Where once, summer-born, with breasts of oranges,
Ripe as the South, the Poontang Princesses
Received their subjects—honey-breath of the hay
Won from the humming coulees, coiled from between their thighs.
Locked in the old dark now.

                              In the white albums, the bare
Bone-farms of the moon, the homesteads gleamed and gloomed.
Coyotes . . .
                      The white night-hunting owl . . .
—Home then. In the fox-prowling,
In the dog-barking, and daylight-seeming night.

2.

The house was thick with the cold wool of their sleep.
In the dark of the kitchen woodbox one cricket sang,
Gold ember of autumn, hung in the christmasy night,
All metal and leather . . .

Cal's lost country.

Then from the top-floor weather, down stairs as limber as rope
My brothers came: Jim, Joe, Martin—Jack as round as sleep,
His head as rough as a corncob—blinking like coons
In the hunters light;
                    And my sister Kathy, my mother—
All sprung out of the dream-encompassing dark
Like need or terror.
Then, in the topaz pool of the lamp's warm solstice,
They dreamed me home
                    Showed me the cloudy pebble,
Pointed to moss on the north of the steering pine,
Gave back my name . . .
                    Chipping the ice of distance from my tongue.

3.

Fiesta then;—the midnight supper
Bright ceremony of the voyager's return.
The cricket sang in the woodbox behind the stove
And the coffee clucked with its black voice.
Their heads nodding on the branch of sleep,
The kids nibbled their dream-cake.
I remember the pearl
Rounds of the sandwich onions (O asphodel
In Elysia!), and the thick and crumbly slabs of the home-made bread,
And the cat's-cradle of talk
As warm as wool, brighter than colored yarn.
Then I was home and it was time for sleep
The kids went up to the dark.
My mother stopped me.
"It's the way the times are Tom. Everyone's broke.
But next year the crops . . . next year, if there's rain . . ."
"Can't be bad times forever," my father said.
"Between them Washington goddamned politicians,
Bankers and debts—they turn a man anyway but loose.
Grasshoppers, rust and dust storms, mortgages and foreclosures,
But we'll make it, Oldtimer. We'll make her yet."
"It's all right," I said. I knew I was home then—
Back and busted from another of my universities.

Night now.

                                       The breathing dark.

The icy room full of dream,

                                           hung with my brothers'

Sleep.

                                  Cold incantations of coyotes

Whine and shine on the bare
Hills.

                              In the dark glitter of the coulee draw
The moon is trapped in the ice.

                                   Away to the north,
Stark in the pouring light, on a page of snow,
The black alphabet of a farm lies jumbled together
Under its blue spike of smoke.

The coulee is full of moonlight: it pours that water
South toward the river dark.

                                   I have come home
From the river. Come up the coulee, come past
The buckbrush breaks where the rabbits lurch and leap,
Where the hunting hawks of the summer make their kill,
Past the Indian graves and home.
How far was the river? In that lunar glaze
In a light as of bone suns I saw on the coulee hills
The long procession of my pawky selves:
My journeying small souls: helved, greaved and garlanded
With the blue weather and the bronze all-favoring
Light of those first fine summers.

                                   Saw, behind,
The daffy caucus of gopher-hunters and swimmers:
Walking delegates to the ego's founding convention:
Runaways
                Shapes out of sleep
                          Voyagers . . .

How far to the river?

                          Perhaps I had never reached it . . .
Never came back; never left . . .
And now returned in the long cortege of myselves.

And now the wind lifts, and I hear the sift of the snow,
A breathing whisper, a steady seethe like the sea
In the shifting porches of pelagic night.

—Went toward a sound of water . . .

                              Called by what bird?
At five I started walking toward my birth,
Working my way toward the water sound and the sound
Of the round song, the water-borne distant singing
Where man chants like a bird in the brilliant bony
Lightening of his tree.

The river is frozen, the moon is caught in the ice.

Returned, now. Home and alone and himselves and warm.
But returned.
                    Alone.
                              Alive, alive oh!
Night of the solstice now, when the long neck of the dark
Leans out of the sun, shadowing the north earth,
The precinct of the Goat.

                              Far from the summer queens
From the golden buttocks, from the high, thrusting thighs
Of last year's girls.

                              Far from my sleeping brothers
In the middle of the journey, returned. Shipwrecked
In the snow of the north forty . . .

                              Drifting . . .
In Capricorn.

              Mac, the double Gladys, Cal, my hope
Swing round my sleep their constant zodiac.

It is far to the river, it is farther home.

The wind is sharpening its knife on the shakes of the roof
              Far

                    Dark

                         Cold
I am a journey toward a distant wound.

VII

1.

Nightmare, nightmare, struggle, despair and dream . . .

The narrow world and the wain swing round my winter sleep . . .

Under the Scorpion's weight my garden flows
Into the dark of the year.

                                 First Neighbor, lately
On strike, calls from his yard to Second Neighbor,
Raking the fallen leaves.

                           Calls, and I hear
The voice of my brother call through the river trees,
Through my nine dead seasons of loss and the frost-bound echoing dusk
Where the gat-toothed buzz-saw burred, a whine and a whicker,
And the round of the oak stump smoked on the freezing ground.

The rusty ports of the sun and no slice of moon in my pocket!
A cold winter that one, as long as absence is,
As white as hunger, a blizzard of lost identities,
When moss grew thick on the south sides of the farmers
And the quick felt of an old and abstract snow
Capped their Rolandic Fissures.

                        Winter under your hat!
A ten year snow-fall under the dome of your head!
You have to split plenty of kindling to warm up from that!

So, that winter, we got wood up from the river
While the migrant bourgeois of Morehead slalomed south on their
                 chins
And my auld acquaintance broke like a covey of quail
And rode the rods to Detroit or soonered westerly—
The Lares half-hitched to the buck jumping Ford—
In a cloud of bankers like Siberian wolves
Snapping at ninety-ninth mortgages tossed like brides in their wake.
Over the hills and far away

To the golden apples of the Oregon.

That's how I saw my boyhood disappear
In a used-up Ford on Highway Number Ten
Toward Devil's Lake and land's end. Vanished. Gone
Toward the apple tree, the singing and the gold.
And my midnight riders gone, the sweet girls of my hunger,
Toward the broad rivers and the ripe and fruited vines,
Coals to Newcastle in the incontinent long winter
Whose cold made your balls ache when there was nothing to warm
But my burning and stallion need—that grand old religion
Of which I am the Pope.

So, entered the dimension of winter, zero of hope
And the only shelter the lee of a barb wire fence.

And far from the laughter.
Far from the high passes.

2.

Beginning and re-beginning, voyage and return and voyage . . .
Past the last gate in the fence toward the white slate of the river,
And past the Indian boneyard and under its tight, bright blanket,
And down the coulee and over the ford, now locked in its echo chamber—
It spanged like gunshot under the caulks of the horseshoes,
A ripping and fiery sound (the pure steel of the cold)
That ricocheted from the hills and sifted snow from the branches,
Unfurling one rusty crow, his sooty flag, to the air.

Stump ranchers that winter, we felled the trees on the slopes,
Scrub-oak, elm, box elder, the flinty stakes of the ash
That snagged in the chokecherry slashes. In the crowded gooseberry brakes,
Where the fox grape's bronze globes sag in the cloudy green of the summer,
We knocked them down with a crosscut and snaked them out on a
                                                        chain.

All that winter, in the black cold, the buzz-saw screamed and whistled,
And the rhyming hills complained. In the noontime stillness,
Thawing our frozen beans at the raw face of a fire,
We heard the frost-bound tree-boles booming like cannon,
A wooden thunder, snapping the chains of the frost.

Those were the last years of the Agrarian City
City of swapped labor
Communitas
Circle of warmth and work
Frontier's end and last wood-chopping bee
The last collectivity stamping its feet in the cold.

So, with the moss on our backs and it snowing inside our skulls,
In a gale like a mile-high window of breaking glass
We snaked out the down ones, snatching the deadfalls clean
And fed them into the buzzsaw.
                           The Frenchman's, it was.
A little guy, quick as a fart and no nicer,
Captain of our industry.
                         Had, for his company
The weedy sons of midnight enterprise:
Stump-jumpers and hog-callers from the downwind counties
The noonday mopus and the coffee guzzling Swedes
Prairie mules
Moonfaced Irish from up-country farms
Sand-hill cranes
And lonesome deadbeats from a buck brush parish.

So, worked together. Fed the wood to the saw
That had more gaps than teeth. Sweated, and froze
In the dead-still days, as clear as glass, with the biting
Acetylene of the cold cutting in through the daylight,
And the badman trees snapping out of the dusk
Their icy pistols.
                    So, worked, the peddlers pack of us
Hunched in the cold with the Frenchman raging around us
A monsoon of fury, a wispy apocolypse, scolding
Cursing and pleading, whipping us into steam,

And we warmed in each others work, contestants of winter,
We sawed up the summer into stove-length rounds—
Chunks of pure sunlight made warmer by our work.
And did we burn?
We burned with a cold flame.
And did we freeze?
We froze in bunches of five.
And did we complain?
We did, we did, we did.

Sometimes at evening with the dusk sifting down through the trees
And the trees like a smudge on the white hills and the hills drifting
Into the hushed light, into the huge, the looming, holy
Night;—sometimes, then, in the pause and balance
Between dark and day, with the noise of our labor stilled,
And still in ourselves we felt our kinship, our commune
Against the cold.
                    In that rich and friendly hour
When the hunting hawks whirred home, we stilled our talking
And silence sang our compline and vesper song.

It was good singing, that silence. From the riches of common work
The solidarity of forlorn men
Firm on our margin of poverty and cold:
Communitas
Holy City
Laughter at forty below
Round song
The chime of comradeship that comes once maybe
In the Winter of the Blue Snow.

That's how it was.

                         Sometimes, going home in the evening,
We'd jump some pheasants and drop them out of the light—
The shotguns clapping and hollow in the empty world of the winter—
And their feathers blazed like jewels in the blank white fields.

Then, if there was plenty, we'd all eat together
At someone's house, and later play poker, for cigarettes or for nothing,

And I'd go home at the dark prime, the north flashing its teeth,
Or the moon white as a lamp in the blazing night.

3.

The moon fattens and fails. In the roaring wood fires
The winter burnt out. One day we stood in the blizzard
Blind as bats in the white rasp of the snow—
In the pure rage of the season one instant—the next,
(With never a slackening of wind or break in the storm)
White turned black and the perfect fury of dust
Slammed down a lid on the day.
                              Montana . . .
                                        Saskatchewan

Blowing over our heads
Buried alive standing up . . .
                                        Still walking around.

Holy Mother of Christ what a pisscutter Spring!
Oxymoronic winter! Anagoge of the snow,
A perfect Red Peril and Jukes of a season
With a muzzle velocity six times the speed of light—
In those days you could be fishing around in a pot-hole
Where a horse or a tractor had sprung a leak and submerged,
Up to your ass in the water, and the rain falling:
And the dust blowing down your throat like a fistful of glass—
And *that* not so bad, but pushing down on your hat
Were the vagrant farms of the north: Montana, Saskatchewan,
With the farmers still on them, merrily plowing away,
Six inches over your head . . .

And *that* not so bad, except for them singing.
So, Spring didn't come. Didn't come for ten years . . .
A simple failure of light in the ice-bound, rusty
Ports of the sun.
                    But I would be sailing out.
Called by what bird? Toward what high pass, in the night,
In the bright blank of my future? Of that white chapter
What did I hope?

In the snowy evening, coming back from the hills
Or walking home after midnight under the tormenting moon
I lugged my brass grief, an unappeasable hunger,
Nameless.
                        Stood in the north Forty,
With no tradition to warm me, demanding a name,
Needing a word for the Now . . . to nail its hide to the barn . . .
Needing to journey . . .

Exile begins early in my country
Though the commune of gentle wood choppers be never so wide and warm.

In the language of water there is no word for fire.

So, carried my anguish around like a poem cast
In bronze:
                        Where verdigris grew like moss on a standing stone,
And sometimes I read its name in the flowing tree of the North,
The midnight river of boreal light.
                                        In the screel of snow
And the iron singing of the wheels of the gravel wagons
Where the WPA farmers worked on the roads
Sometimes I seemed to hear.
                        Immortal
Loneliness
                                Shapes of the dark
                                                Cold
Partners.
This song the old moon sang me, coming home in the night.
And the icy tongues of the stars.

After Christmas.
                Drifting
Toward the Water Carrier . . .

                        —Sang me toward sleep.

And out on the hills one coyote . . .

                                Barking his lauds . . .

VIII

"Expropriate the expropriators—that's Marx. But Plato's guardians
Might not eat off gold plate."

                                        Hovey is speaking
Muttering, low voiced, in the funky dark.
I hush him quiet, whispering, hearing
A papery rustle of onions, a surd trill
And a thudding and sighing collapse, the waltz of potatoes
As the pile slides. Then they tick in the sack.

"All property is theft. By stealing Prexy's potatoes,
Behold, I'm become a man of property."
I say nothing, fishing around in the dark
For the slippery onions that peel themselves in my grasp.
I feel the push of the wind on the low-slung roof,
The sound distant, like far trains, like the sea
Shoving its thunder inland.

"Stealing is better done without philosophy."
I tell him. He mutters. Light leaps out of his hand
And the root-cellar lifts around us its solid arms.
"Turnips" he says and points to a far corner.
"Third ingredient, the philosopher's stone, the magus
Of all stews. Get some."

                                        The match goes out
And I fill the sack by feel in the darkness under
The earth; in the warm and vegetable dark
I mend my philosophy, stealing pieces of night,
Out of the press of the long storm.

Outside, the wind still pushed its heavy freight
South. The cold laced at our throats. The night
Boomed down from the north. A hang-dog moon
Was racing about in the clouds, and a rapid branch
Of music bloomed at the President's window, its flowers

Flapping loose in the gale.

We went, then, over the swell and swale
Of the campus back-lots, past the dwellings of Greeks,
Their monogramed houses founded on light and their lawns
Crew cut. We passed the creek and came out
At the railroad siding.

                                    The raw edge of a fire
Rubbed at the windy dark. One old tramp in his hunger
Jungling up in the cold. Bummed us. We gave him
A part of what we had stolen, and made for Camp.

2.

Camp Depression!
               O smallest particular
In the chilly universality of want!
Pustulant diamond hung on the pure brow
Of our golden west!

                             O bob-tailed quiddity,
Earnest of earnest compromise with the cold,
With the entropy of the failing system!
Now, under the northwest wind, in the first snow of the season,
We enter the ring of light.

                                  A string of cabooses
Remnants of vanished trains, crouch in a square
Like the pioneers' covered wagons, a tight perimeter
Against the Comanche winter.

                                   I came with our stolen grub
Into the cooking stink and twitch of talk . . .

                                 —Crossed the high passes,
Came to the named pool, to the omen stone.

That's how I got there, finally, to Grand Forks
In North Dakota, to the University there,
And to Camp Depression, with a few potatoes and onions
Out of the President's cache.
                               O impeccable faubourgs
Where, in the morning, you fought bedbugs, for your shoes!

Implacable need:

                             the search for the blazed tree,
And the long and lonely hunt for the naming rune—
In that legendary journey so early and hard begun
Toward joy, toward the laughter, I was no longer alone
In that cantrip circle, in the bright chime of their talk
Among those pilgrim souls.
Wendell I see, wearing the dog on his back,
And Weston comes in with the snow, with the howling night,
And Sorensen, with his clenched face, and his hard
Opinions.
         And all the others.

                        Shapes of the dark

Faces
Blown to windward
Blown past our head-lights
Proofs
Of a lost, ebullient season.
Time has its tin ear, history drops at your gate its yellowing gazettes . . .
Off-beat functions, seasons too soon or too late
Begun.
                    It was that sort of time. It was not
The Year of the Blue Snow.
But we couldn't have known it, plucked from the sweat of our sleep
In the north Forty . . . blown out of spring toward
The steep of winter, the metaphysical cold.

We talked to keep warm (and made love, even, alas,
To keep warm). My vision of everything flat
The ninety-nine mile shelf of books, the sledding fathers
Touring south on their beards—in the smell of hunger,
In the small eye of a rifle six years unmade
The talk flickered like fires.
The gist of it was, it was a bad world and we were the boys to change it.
And it *was* a bad world; and we might have.

In that round song, Marx lifted his ruddy
Flag; and Bakunin danced (And the Technocrats

Were hatching their ergs . . .)

                                A mile east, in the dark,
The hunger marchers slept in the court house lobby
After its capture: where Webster and Boudreaux
Bricklayer, watchmaker, Communists, hoped they were building
The new society, inside the shell of the old—
Where the cops came in in the dark and we fought down the stairs.

That was the talk of the states those years, that winter.
Conversations of east and west, palaver
Borne coast-to-coat on the midnight freights where Cal was riding
The icy red-balls.
                  Music under the dogged-down
Dead lights of the beached caboose.
Wild talk, and easy enough now to laugh.
That's not the point and never was the point.
What was real was the generosity, expectant hope,
The open and true desire to create the good.

Now, in another autumn, in our new dispensation
Of an ancient, man-chilling dark, the frost drops over
My garden's starry wreckage.
                      Over my hope.
                              Over
The generous dead of my years.
                        Now, in the chill streets
I hear the hunting, and the long thunder of money.
A queer parade goes past: Informers, shit-eaters, fetishists,
Punkin-faced cretins, and the little deformed traders
In lunar nutmegs and submarine bibles.
And the parlor anarchist comes by, to hang in my ear
His tiny diseased pearls like the guano of meat-eating birds.
But *then* was a different country, though the children of light,
                                gone out
To the dark people in the villages, did not come back . . .
But what was real, in all that unreal talk
Of ergs and of middle peasants (perhaps someone born
Between the Mississippi and the Rocky Mountains, the unmapped country)

Was the generous wish.

                       To talk of the People
Is to be a fool. But they were the *sign* of the People,
Those talkers.

                       Went underground about 1941
Nor hide nor hair of 'em since; not now, in the Year
Of the Dog, when each hunting hound has his son of a bitch.
Their voices got lost in the rattle of voting machines
In the Las Vegas of the national politic . . .

4.

We go out in the stony midnight.

                   Meridian cold.

                     The stars,
Pure vitriol, framed in the blank obsidian dark,
Like skaters icy asterisks; smolder; and sing; and flame.
In the flickering light, auroral, of the North lifting its torch,
The stacks of the powerhouse fume and sigh. . .

                        High up, streaking
The lower dark, the smoke whisks east in the slack of a cranky breeze.
A train mourns. Distant. A broken fifth of its spoor
Crowns the brow of the night with its wild mystique.
And under the hysteria of the time, its blind commitments,
Is the talk and electric whisper of the power
Loud in forgotten counties where the poor
Sharpen their harps and axes in the high shine of the dark.

That was our wintry idyl, our pastorale in the cold.
The train whistle for the journey, the smoking stacks for power,
And in every country the need and the will to change.
O landscape of romance, all iron and sentiment
Under the prose of snow!

Later, crossing the black yards of the campus,
We heard the dead cry out from the long marble of sleep—
The old heads of the past, a-dream in their stony niches,
Above their Latin Wisdom.

                    Being classical—

In the teeth of the northwest wind.

                                        The old dead, and the dead
Still walking around.

I saw all that as the moon spun down toward the Badlands
In the singing cold that only our blood could warm.
A dream surely. Sentimental with its
Concern for injustice (which no one admits can exist).
And some of them died of it, giving blood to the dream.
And some of them ran away; and are still running.

And it's all there, somewhere.

                                        Under the hornacle mine . . .
In the tertiary deposits . . .

                        —Ten minutes before the invention of money . . .

IX

1.

--- and the moon stuck in my pocket!
And all my infernal suns shining against the cold!

Now, what is harder to know than the simplest joy?
Under the lacing of anger and of lack,
In the rub of hunger, in the thick hug of the dark,
What brightness, sweetness, softness can we know?
What road to the honey tree?
        Sweetness falls,
A hawk from broad heaven sweet in his swift kill.
Softness grows on stone in the mossy watches
Its hardness keeps. And asleep in the shape of a cloud,
A brightness waits and leaps.
        Hawk, cloud, stone—
Pure marvel, here, this brightness, sweetness, softness.

   The stars are shifting in the permanent sky . . .
   Yellow Arcturus—
   That star, my lifetime of light away, leans down the sleepy west,
   Bright on the lifting lilac.
       Our fellow of scars and wars
   Drifting, old Earth, into the shine of the spring
   Toward the stone-footed Ram and the Bull . . .

Marvel me no marvels: that lightness, softness, sweetness
Is no marvel.
      Blood comes from a stone,
Night is the shining weather in which the blind go hunting,
But that all-purpose dark in which we seek our good
Works from its black double, as night breaks into day
And the sleepy opposite wakes.
       There is no marvel here
Where we get our blood from a stone, beating our hands at the wall.

No, but the pure joy, then; simple: got without effort.

Born without categories it puts the skids under
The blind eye of the moon—it jumps all fences.
It was she had it—Marian—a small slice of the sun
No bigger than the half of an orange—it was what the sun keeps warm by—
A rose, a flower of warmth in the heart of the abstract cold.
I was bound to lose it.

     The stars shift in the stony sky
     Arcturus
     Drifting . . .
     Bootes the Herdsman

               Chasing the Bear with his dogs.

A warmth, a sunlight, and an end of journies—
That's what she seemed like, was;
Or the permanent sky, maybe,

           myself drifting,

                   or flame
Would light me north in the long collapse of Time
When Vega is pole star.

So the journey ended, or seemed to, in the sweet strength of her flesh,
That brightness . . . softness . . .

              in the fire-flame, in the fixed cone
Of light, I broke my fast, I woke my want.

The simplest joy!
          And there is no way to say it!

Only that the birds in the boondocks hoisted my heart in their song.
Only that trees, only that the damn-all flowers
That work for no one, that wink their yellowy talk
Flag right, flag left, hallooing from field to field
Their breezy semiphores—only that the wind, the rain
Under my skin of names, the St. Elmo's fire,
The fur of my sensual animal, touched the quick of my ghost.

So, the birds in the boondocks sang.

          And the high-flying moon

Ground round on its bony axis.

                                    My new born interior suns
Warmed all their hands in the single flash of a word;
In my four-alarm song, at the long wick of my joy.

Well, what's the use of talking? It wasn't like that.
And it was, enough. But to put the whole thing down plain,
It was the dancer's bulge in the thick of her calf.
It was a trick of the eye, a way of walking, of saying.
Or it was the shy sound of her talk or a knack for goodness.

None of these things, not one; no way says it.
Was it the flare and bulge of the charmed light as it eased around her,
Bright swarming of sun, like bees, nudging her hair?
It was. It was.
Was it the calloused first joint of her second finger,
Stigmatic short hand, got from the taking of notes?
It was. Christ yes it was.
Was it the young moon in the sign of the first woman
The quail-keeping girl, the girl with the red-eared hound?
It was. It was. It was.
And all thrown away?
It was.

2.

A spitfire oak of thunder, sky-high roots in a cloud,
Strikes down a branch of sound and the season splits like a grape.
The sooty elms, that all blanched winter long
Dragged their slow charcoal through the white brag of the snow
Now shift like smoke in the whelming rain.
                          A light, alive,
Alone:
                          A bright bird.
                          The yellow spike of a flower;
A shimmering haze of willows clots in the greeny light.

In that spring the rusty platitudes brightened
Old axioms of sun and night

The invisible selves under the skin of objects
Singing
Told me their secret numbers and the true count of their names.
So that I saw the snake split the long glove of his home
And go forth all new, man-killing, naked and moist,
Steaming in the cold morning, a smoky ooze through the grass;
And the gold-eyed pheasant leaped out from an ambush of light
Scattering the dew, and with the dew still on his wings,
Beating up tiny rainbows out of his coppery thunder.

      Sun like a gold swarm of bees; moon like a magical woman.
      These things I had once; things that she gave me.

3.

Love and hunger!—the secret is all there somewhere—
And the fiery dance of the stars in their journeying far houses.
And if hunger ended in the cantrip circle,
In the union of hungry men, in the blue ice of the reefer
Where Cal travelled . . .

Jawsmiths
Commune of mystical sweat.
If it ended there.

It was she built the fire in the heart of the winter night
And rang all the bells in the stiff church of the ice.
Miners light:
Campfire:
Chipping hammer of purest flame, tunneling
The ultimate rock, the darkness that is as long as we are . . .

Seemed like no camp fire,
But the permanent warmth, the absolute seed of the sun
I could sow in my personal blood-ranch . . .
But I am a farmer of bones.

      *   *   *   *   *   *

A season was ending.

White papers; architectural changes.

In Whitey's Circular Bar, in East Grand Forks,
We stood like the signal figures under the legend tree,
Drinking. With Sam and Dee. Who were talking of marriage.
Stood in the rain of music and silver under the illegal machines,
Where Alton pursued the mechanical capitalist,
Jacking the slot machine's arm down again and again.

"Marriage is the continuation of sex by other means."
(Sam was going away to drive airplanes for the government.
Someone sang in Norwegian, under the metallic laughter
Of machines and money).

"Some people can be happy with a book by Donne
And a piece of Ass. It's lack of high thought keeps
My life poor."

(And went out in a chiming rain
Of jackpot silver).
And crossed the black river one instant before the breakup.
And turned dreamward.

One to the East and airplanes,

One, Marian to the true North. One
To the West of Wish. Myself, South, toward speech.
And all to the wars and the whores and the wares and the ways of a rotten season.
And who could have guessed it?
The pole star stood to the North:
Fire was steady on the permanent sky.

4.

Then South to the University with the 500,000 pianos
Bought because Huey Long had written: "Get rid of them nags!"
(Horses for the young ladies riding stable)
Because one of the horses had broken the neck of a possible voter.
To Baton Rouge, Louisiana, the University there.
Where they had bought football, pianos, horses and donnish Oxonians.
To start a culture farm, a little Athens-on-the-bayou.
And a good job too.

                                  And they all put in together and they got up
A tradition. They got hold of Donne, and before they had got done
They damn near had him.

                                  And they got hold of Agrarianism—
Salvation—40 acres and a mule—the Protestant Heaven,
Free Enterprise! Kind of intellectual ribbon-development—
But I was a peasant from Sauvequipeuville—
I wanted the City of Man.

And Cleanth Brooks would talk, at the Roosevelt Tavern,
Where we went to drink beer. And Katherine Anne Porter sometimes.
(They've probably changed all the names now.)
And down the street Alan Swallow was handsetting books
In an old garage. A wild man from Wyoming,
With no tradition.

                                  But it came in handy, later,
That tradition. The metaphysical poets
Of the Second Coming had it for God or Sense—
Had it in place of a backbone: and many's the scarecrow,
Many's the Raggedy Man it's propped up stiff as a corpse.

Then, Asia Street: where I roomed at the family Peets.
A bug mine, a collapsible chamber of horrors
Held together by tarpaper and white chauvinism.
There was Peets with his gin, his nine foot wife, and his son
Who was big enough to be twins—and stupid enough for a dozen,
And the daughter, big as all three, with a back-side for a face,
With a mouth of pure guttapercha, with a cast, with a fine
High shining of lunacy crossing her horsy eyes—
"Fuck or fight!" I can hear her yelling it now
And out of the room at the back the bed starts roaring,
The house is moaning and shaking, the dust snows down from the ceiling,
The old dog sneezes and pukes and Peets is cursing his wife:
"Teach your daughter some manners, you goddam cow!
Tell her to close her door, and come back to this goddam bed!"

And Hopkins arrives with his latest girl and *they* start
Kicking the gong around; and the whole place shaking and roaring,
Like a plane about to take off; and the 'gators awake

Bellowing, under the house, and flee for the bayous
While the old dog screams at the moon—
Order! Tradition and Order!
And all the beds in the joint a-flap at both ends!

Then I would get up, maybe, leaving that sex foundry,
That stamping mill for the minting of unfixed forms,
And lug my chastity, my faithfulness, around the town.
Moon in the western dark and the blue permanent stars
Shifted a bit in the sky.
                Toward music, toward speech, drifting
The night.
High noon of darkness now and the loud magnolias lifting
Their ten-thousand candle-power blooms.
              Proud flesh, these flowers,
Earth offering, inescapable
Emblems.
Offering of night birds too, and the travelling far stars
And the round dance of the seasons: inviolate
Torment.

Open the night's cold book.
              Salt for the quick.
Now from the farthest bar a music breaks and binds,
An icy necklace of bluest fire spills down the hour.
The river stirs and seethes, its steady working whispering
Into the ultimate South.
           Drifting
Toward Scorpio in the hangdog heat of the sullen season.
Toward the Gulf . . .
In the river-run hush and hurry of that great night water:
To the black lots and the god-mating beasts of the green man-farming sea.

5.

Living again on the outside—that's what it was.
—Outside of the Outside: drinking beer with a comrade,
A Negro guy, in a Negro bar—put into the kitchen

(Business being business, whether white or black).
And plenty of reason, God knows, two blocks away
From higher education.

                           Which was the Roosevelt Tavern,
Brooks, that sweet great man, K.A.P. etc.
(They've changed all the names now).

                               And all of them
On Donne. Etc.
            And all of them sailing on the Good Ship Tradition . . .
For the thither ports of the moon.

                          High flying days
I'll tell you right now!
                 And me with my three ideas
With my anarchist, peasant poverty, being told at last how bright
The bitter land was.
How the simple poor might lift a laud to the Lord.

That's how it was. Geeks, Cons and Lemon Men,
Guys with their intellects all ganted up out of the barbarian North
Tea sluggers and cathounds
The girl who, when I said that God had created
Male and female the Spanish Moss, wanted to see them in action:
People "with a groundless fear of high places."
O architectonic colloquoy! O gothick Pile
Of talk! How, out of religion and poetry
And reverence for the land the good life comes.
Some with myth, some with Visions out of
That book by Yeats would dance the seasons round
In a sweet concord.
                        But never the actual seasons—
Not the threshing floor of Fall nor the tall night of the Winter—
Woodcutting time—nor Spring with the chime and jingle
Of mended harness on real and farting horses,
Nor the snort of the tractor in the Summer fallow.
Not the true run of the seasons.

That year they set up machine guns down at the docks
To quarantine a seaman's strike.

                                    And Warren went, by mistake,
Being new in the town, to the fink hall, looking
For the strike committee.
                                    Got dumped. That was the year
They knocked off Carey, who edited the Gulf Pilot.
M_____ did it; who's now a great leader of men.

Serious talk, all of it. Serious people.
"The difference between lust and love is the difference between
Power and knowledge."
                                    And Warren talks of
General strikes, Anarcho-Communist notions,
Picked up in Wobbly stewpots.
                              "Stick out your behind to the North
Wind and see which cheek gets cold first," Peets says.
"Know thyself" he confides. "In the dark, a wise man
Can tell his ass from his elbow."

Palaver—
Tradition! Heigh ho! Tradition!
Bobbery! Bobbery. Palaver—

DON'T GO BAREFOOT TO A SNAKE-STOMPING!
                              LOOSEN YOUR WIGS!

It's no use hooking them both on the same circuit—
The English and American traditions.
It won't take the play out of the loose eccentrics.
Cattlemen, sheepmen and outlaws, that's American writing,
And few enough outlaws at that.
                                    And it's no use
For the lonesome radicals to raise up the ghost of Tom Paine,
Los Muertos no hablan
                              Them dead don't walk, either.
                              No, ghost-eaters, they'd like
To cuddle up to the bourgeois liberal tradition—

Go to bed to make love, not to keep warm!
I'll gentle my own horses.

63

Now come down from your mountain Master Don
          Gordon
All's dark down here.
                    Asia Street.
                              Marsh Street.
                                        My garden
Dreams in my window light.
                    Somewhere—toward morning—
Is the true anguish and body of a man . . .
Buried in all that talk.
                    Come down and find him.

          *   *   *   *   *

Stars in the night sky anyway, even though shifted.
To go out then, in the dark, leaving the talkers behind,
Tapping my stick of light on the smooth face of the road
To stir the snakes.
                    They came up out of the inky swamps
To soak up heat from the black-top in the long chill of the night,
Cottonmouths.
          Lay there like logs of wood,
                              Sluggish, huddles of
Older darkness.
                    And out of the further night
The black rush and the voiceless hurrying call
Of the great beast of the river.
                              Pushing south
Toward the long coilings of the labyrinthine Gulf.

Then home to Asia Street and the family Peets
The knocking-shop and threshing floor of love
Now roaring and shaking on the two o'clock jump.
A conversation of parts. Another tradition.
And someone is saying
"Sex plus electrification equal socialism."

                              6.
First the talk, and after the talk the gunfire.

After the hunt, with music, you walk back, avoiding the snakes,
To the shaking loud house, your hireling momentary home,
Through the crowding invisible snow and the quick ice of the times.
Low temperatures there! Winter still in the streets—
(Where Morehead's migrant fathers, still belly down on the roads,
Their beards stiffer than boards, sledded past and around me,
Heading toward deeper Souths).

                        Winter of Winters:
40 below Mason Dixon and the gauge still falling,
The pressure rising, the middle sliding out toward the edges—
Place where the blacker the man the brighter he burns;
And the hotter the fire the colder.

I left there then and hitched north in summer on the black roads through the swamps:
Water hyacinths; and moss fogged trees; and the soft thick rasp of snakes
And flamingos on their thin stalks like passion aloft in a breeze
Heraldic emblems.

And on north then with the first of the Dog Faces
(Who thought they were National Guardsmen) done with maneuvers
In Louisiana; heading for home in the North; and now
Rotten these many years.
                    North, past the turpentine
Camps of Arkansas, past the decayed, decaying
Limestone of the Ozarks.
                  North toward Bonne Terre—
(Missouri: the flat north; wooded: the chat heaps from the mines
Where they made cement) toward Marian and a kind of Red
Wedding.
                Count of my name, number
Of my secret beast
All true marriages are sacred and shake the King of the Year
Out of his sleepy past . . .
                  No—it was only
How to be happy.
(They've changed all the names; those systems are *long* forgotten,
But that's what it was).

We lodged among madmen. The rain dripped through the roof
And my great toe turned to limestone—another story.
Later, by way of honeymoon, went to the nameless river,
Swam there.
                    (Treeful of quarreling squirrels.)
                                        The holy man
Who never returned from Oran (remained alive there)
And his sweet wife.
                                Stayed there by the river,
In the half-life of a wet-wood fire, while the night
Seeped upward out of the ground.
                                        Yet the light hung still
On the steep hill faces, in the long west sky; at tree top
It graced the birds' high houses.

It was then we heard the hounds and the sound of the hunt coming—
A far belling of dogs and a quick rustle of darkness,
And then all still.
                        The trees leaned up toward the light, the river
Dreamed on a stone.
                        Then, through the eldritch tranced and dying light,
Like the quick of the falling dark, from a brake of willow,
A swift flicker of drawn-out speed, night's Presence leaped.
He splashed through the river shallows, a buck, running, while three
Low melancholy keenings came from the distant hounds.

Then came the long night running by the river shallows:
Pursuit
Workings of darkness
The endless hunting.
Deer, their shapes like smoke, with their flaring eyes
Flowed out of the rising dark. Delicate, slight,
With the bitten-in red glare to her glance, and lightly stepping
The fox came, trotting easy for the length of the long running.
And the pigs came, bustling and scuffling in a storm of terror,
And the wild cats from the trees like fur on springs,
And the small thin things from the brush, and the stroller, the disdainful badger,
Rolling out of the dark—everything running, running—
The night running, the darkness alive with

Running and the terror of the long running.

The brush cracked like shot and the great shapes leaped,
Rode by like cloud, their eyes slashed long by speed,
In a great frieze of terror.
The great and the noble deer and the poor weak things of the dark
Running, running, the hills wild with their terror
The brush smashing and rustling and the shallows patterned with splashes—
Till the whole world seemed running in that long hunt.
And the tame cattle joined the running, came bellowing out of
    the brush
Their holy terror, their anguished disbelief that they were hunted;
The horses crashed by, screaming their hurt and hatred,
And the barnyard geese, and the very birds of the place—
And at the last a man—was it a man?
Came out of the willow brake, running without a sound
While the pealing keen of the hounds grew iron and round on the hills.
It passed us running, a thing of the purest night,
Soundless.
     The terrible eyes begged no release.

Then the shadowy great figures, the long night running,
The night-long frieze like cloud or cloudy terror
Vanished beyond the river and the silence came.
Dead silence. No
Leaf fall or cricket-cry. Even the river
Stilled.

Then we smelled them—the fierce, sickening dog-smell,
The stench of their long pursuit.
     And the huge forms come padding
Stinking, red-eyed out of the old dark.
We lay there by the small fire and they watched us,
Knowing, unhurried.

Then the hunt went on—
We heard it vanish past the farthest hill.
The night came back—the leaves were clashing
Their little leathery swords. A sleepy bird

Complained.
And, as the hunt grew still in the distant running
We made love there, hearing the farthering hounds.

7.

The stars shift and maps are redrawn: of islands
Blown up at sea, of frontiers soft as chalk,
Of archipelagos adrift, blazing, and facades of cathedrals
Famous . . .

           Redrawn in fire . . .

                    As I went toward the North
Europe bled and burned. For each state line that I crossed
Nations were sold and collapsed.

                 They died in the oily smoke
Of the high summer—the poor—

               died out in the country
Which before they'd never had money enough to see.

"Last year" said old Tom Brennan; "They made me dance to their tune.
Labor was scarce and they had me over a barrel.
This year I'll fire the bastards at the drop of a hat.
By God, I'll keep the roads black with 'em!"

And the roads *were* black with men. Toward Fresno, toward Dijon
Toward Terre Haute, Bonne Terre, toward Paris, toward Warsaw, toward
Medicine Hat the roads were alive.

                    Refugees
International winter:
The long night-running toward another shore.

Yet, in the shifting light, love seemed enough:
By the wavering fire as the long hunt went by us.
And seemed enough as I hitch hiked north in the heavy summer
Through the Kansas wheat, toward the rust-red roaring harvest of the high North—
Enough to sale *love*: and all those masterless men
To become their masters in the commune of mystical toil:
Round-dance:
Lauds toward a newer sun.

But no one said love.

     Toward Bonne Terre, toward Reno, Lands End—
Or if it was said no one heard in the long running.

Still, it *was* said. We said it, if no one heard it.
And, going north through the summer in what was the end of a life
(Though it seemed a beginning) the crazy jungles, the wild
People on the roads—*that* was my true country:
And still is so—the commune: of pure potential.

To be in love, then, was a desperate business.
Marvellous. It was to stand with a Dechard rifle
Against the charge of the Ogallah Sioux.
It was a pledge to revolts that never come.
It guaranteed a future that could not exist.
And so many were in love then. Really in love. Curious—
Like a disease . . .

     The life of a dangerous time.

8.

North to Maine, then.

     Past my home, with the ghosts
Loud in the house: loud by the river and all else fading, fading
As if to be ghosts.

     But it was myself was fading,
My number up, the summer falling away
Toward the crowding war and the gay and calling host of the dead
Who laughed all around me.

The road lead direct into the landscape of dream:
Bird-song and water-sound and the north coil of the rivers
Beyond height of land.

     And the long pines leaning down
Under Canadian winds.

     And the trapped lakes, lost
Under the green night and the steady whispering weight
Of the unsleeping trees.

Waterville Maine, the coil of the Kennebec
The stars fixed forever in the winter ice.

It seemed so.
                    In the frozen purity of the long northern night,
Hearing the high pipes and the wild drumming, continuous,
Loud, of the Syrian (or Armenian) workers' . . .
Alien song that was: a wintry hieroglyph
Hung in the ear of night like a freight train whistle
Strange and familiar. Hearing that song the unfixed
World turned round and steadied. I heard again the old
Song, in that circle where solidarity and the obscene
Lie down like the lamb and the lion.

In the college I taught in, too: the familiar—
Hank, Bill, Jim—the second order rebellion.
The cantrip circle where wish is king of the woods.

And beyond that to the Old China Hands of that province:
Christers from Little East Jesus Falls, from West Burlap,
From Unity, Chastity and Modest Bastardy, Maine;
And the faculty members, each of them riding fence
On some King Ranch of the intellect: Texas talkers,
With running irons in their soogans and an eye for the maverick dogie
Of a new thought: would slap their brands on fast
And next Fall sell it up-river, to the slaughter-house pens of the North.

The same old jazz: North Dakota with pine trees
And the coiling rivers. Hunger alive in the compounds
Where the workers sang, the Wish prowling the streets
Where the jobless demonstrated under the icons
Of Its insurrectionary Name.
Potential—our love seemed to insure it . . .

9.

Stars in the black ice, fixed, and the shining figures
Swing through their formal houses. The long pond spangs and crackles
Under our flashing skates—a zodiac of my loves

70

Rings round the drowning stars . . .
                              Periphery, periphery—
                              How shall we say that brightness trapped in the black ice?

Item:
The one with the beard was Hank, who was proving something
With starfish he cut up in his own apartment
And the place stank of them. Also of hot buttered rum.

Item:
The aimless Finn, the organizer frozen to death on a freight—
Somewhere beyond Bangor—"whose name I cannot remember."

                      Periphery   periphery
Item:
Mrs. Mintz with her watery, no-color eyes,
Like those of some unclassified bird and her hoarse croak.
Had lost her voice selling bread which she lugged through the streets—
The great black loaves of the rye as hard as stones
In the bright cold.
                      Had a suitor
A junk man from Concord who sold scrap iron to Japan,
Who coveted her mortgaged house.
                                    He came one day, bearing
The gift of a chicken and demanding a straight answer
To his modest proposal.
                      She said no.
                                    Thereupon
He divided the chicken in half and went on his way. Proper
Bostonian.

We had an apartment in that same mortgaged house:
Chandelier like a landslide on the Glass Mountain,
A great brass bed that seemed to be hung with bells.
All winter long, in the apocalyptic night—
The wolves howling at the edge of the pines, the Armenians singing,
Hank explaining his starfish, the wars sharpening their knives,

And Mrs. Mintz, like a mad saint, proferring bread in the streets—
All the wild dark, invincibly riding toward sleep,
We sang our love like a four-alarm fire. We rode past
Auroral midnights like Lapland majesty.

Then, Spring. The shifting light altered
The shapes of the hills. The hollows ponded with sifting
Sun and the small lakes filled with the tall, fallen, meridian
Blue.
        And in fence corners where, in the rainy autumn
I found the secret fruit, the winy, wind-downed cold
Apples—green shoots! now, of the hyacinth.
Daffodil, pickerel weed in the ponds, in the sedgy shallows;
And coppery crowds of the willow clouding the rivers' edge.

And all new! New as the black snake under
The winter house of his skin!
And the first true warmth in the blue thunder, the light.

These things I had once. This brightness, softness, sweetness
She gave me once to my keeping.
Piece of the true sun.

*　　*　　*　　*　　*

Then the bird sang down his loud and ignorant note
And the stars were shifted in their fiery towns:
Arcturus:
Trapped in the lilac:
And I went south, by the coiling Kennebec river
 (While the still stones sang, and the trees—and that free idiot bird—
Of the joys of the season)
Went with password forgotten—and the moon stuck in my pocket!
Toward War and the City;
Toward cold change and the anonymity of number:
Down river, down river,
Toward the bone-cold, wrestling coils of the salt, dumb-foundering sea.

X

1.

"Put me down God," Preacher Noone says. "Put me down.
Here am I, 10,000 miles up and I'm flyin' blind;
Got no wings, got no airplane, got no passport—I say to you, **God,**
Put me down, sir."

The stormy midnight. A scatter of stars scuds north
Under the rip-tooth clouds.

                               The little lost towns go by,
Towns of the dark people: a depot, a beer joint, a small
Fistful of lights flung East as the red-ball train goes past.

So we went north, taking a trip toward a war,
A long picnic, a sleep-out three years long, a regular pisscutter,
Went through the town of Buffalo, where once, with my father,
We stopped in the eye of a dust storm and I heard
The rattling freight go by.

                               Went through there now—
Whistling fistful of light blown east toward the morning,
Toward what was becoming our Past—ten miles north of home
And eight years into that older and colder dark
I once was strange to.

("This train ain't bound for glory," says Preacher Noone.
                                  "this train
Ain't bound for glory. Put me down God, please sir.")

History:
          blown past the headlights to windward.

2.

West to Seattle and a cold camp.

                          Got our ship in that harbor,

And the first sailing we did was to circle around for a day
Like an old dog nosing the place he intends to lie down.
Correcting the compass, that was, so we wouldn't sail toward the wrong war.
North, then on the Inside Passage, like a dream of rebirth:
Ocean river between islands, between islands and mountains,
Between waterfalls on the mountains and the cold, exiling sea,
Her green estrangement.

                            Unhurried, out of the night,
The old, great, constellations, the soul-boats and ships of the heroes,
The fiery cities and signatures of the dead—burning—
Sailed up out of the North.

                             And the North itself was blazing,
A cold and prophetic light.

                          By night: that ghost of warmth;
And the days grey as the Host in a pale mizzle of rain,
Transitional.

                There the piled salmon shoaled at stream-mouth,
And the dreamy, fishing bear hoisted the old, melancholy,
Great, hairy, disguising, joke of his head.
He stroked the sea with his enormous paw.
Silver and red the dull light gleamed on the bloodied salmon!
Holding the fish like a flag, he turned us his hooded stare,
Uncaring, alien, wild.
                    The ship sailed past
That massive indifference, into the lagging, transitional, wilderness
Light.

3.

And all toward the wars and the whores and the wares and the ways of a rotten season .
Anchorage, Alaska, a little nugget of dung
Hung in the eye of legend, in the quick-summer ice of gold braid.
There the little war was going forward on schedule:
The citizens, sharpening their knives, were six jumps ahead of
           the soldiers—
They were already living in nineteen ninety. The whores
Were working three rooms at once—for the dressing, the un-
          dressing, and the business,

And the whorehouse lines, past the General's house, went round
                     the block and past
The Athabascan, the Great Slave, past White Horse, Winnipeg,
Past Kalamazoo and Boston, toward Independence Hall,
Where the last yardbird was easing his fly in the cold light
Of the north and towering stars.
                                    There's patriotism for you—
In the black light of the louring midnight sun!

Somehow the Army, those reluctant civilians, sleepwalking
In the bronzy dream of their elders, that khaki expensive night,
Got past the whores and the open doors and the forming fours
And past the true ice of Cook Inlet and the ugly frozen river,
And supply sergeants: offering their tropic equipment.
And took ship again at Seward.

                             ("I give you up, God," says Parson
Noone. "I give you up, Sir. You got me cornered
With a Williwaw roaring around my ass and my pants down—
Doctrinal matters blown past at ninety an hour—
I do hereby give you up, sir, truly.")

Cold Bay, Adak, Sitka, Indifference Bay
The brown mountains, smoky, lifted out of the sea
Burning.
Kulaga. Semisoposhnoi. Dutch Harbor
Where the bombed ships lay rusting like dirty cardboard
Tramped flat in the icy water, and the rats fought at the rat-guards—
There bodies brown as the brown mountains under their moulting
                     fur—
Fought and fell in the freezing urine-colored sea.

Then down the Chain in a five year fog, in a 90 mile wind.
Below decks the crackers (no one went overseas
Except southerners and myself) were cleaning their rifles:
Enfields that hadn't been cleaned since nineteen fourteen,
The bolts rusted tight as a safe.
But now and again they fired them,
The richochets rattling around in those iron kitchens

75

Like angry popcorn.

So: we came to my island:
Called Fireplace, then, in the comfortable code of the admen
Who could send out a flight of children—and shoot them down
            the guns
Of that fiery island Kiska—yes: and call those dead ones home—
Under the name of Rinso White.

                                    It is hard

To die for an adman—

                    Oh Adman Kadman!

Got to Amchitka then, under a yellow alert,
The two planes of the place orbiting, the water gun-colored
In a smoky drizzle of rain.
A miserable, choked-up harbor
So shallow that landing craft went aground and those Misplaced Persons,
Drowned or just too pooped out in the landing, bobbed round
In the mankilling-cold surf: among the orange crates and oil drums
And the sealed filing cases of the people who'd bought the war.
Climbed ashore there, too tired to be scared when the usual Charlie
Came beating his eggs or washing his clothes in the skies
We had never longed for.
                            But there was no war that day.
And we climbed the long hill, through the mud, toward a bed
            in the snow.

4.

Everything externalized; everything on the outside;
Nowhere the loved thing, or the known thing.
In the night of the army, the true sleepwalkers' country
All are masked familiars at the deaths of strangers—
It was the strangeness moved us.
                                In the cold blur of the rain
The bombers call: "Fireplace, Fireplace, do you read me,
Fireplace?"
Call and come in: great truck-loads of the dead,
And the crazy medics, with needles stuck in their arms,
Come down to greet them.

In that country, under the sun-tan statutes of the place,
All death is by accident; and all life is also.
"War is the continuation of life by other means,"
Saith the Preacher (noone). "It's like walking naked
Through the mating grounds of the Buzz Saw in his native habitat,
Its *one side or a leg off.*"
                                        It isn't like that.

No. In the war, if you didn't die, someone
Did your dying for you. It's there the guilt comes—
Nothing chosen and real: only the bombers loading
Reluctant bodies that someone else must shoot at—
Distracting.
                        It was *that* set the poets all wrong,
So that they went off to the war—in their insured opinions—
And (properly bitter) wrote like the minor versers
Of 1916: The one about getting equipment,
The one about firing for score, the one about
The Christian and/or Jew buried "abroad", the one
About the corpse in the green house.
                                —All of it proper, of course,
A good "oppositional" poetry, as if it were made to order.

(Ho! John Thomas! What a sad state you're in now!
Your balls as cold as the brass monkey's, and around your neck
An old zodiac of bombers: falling down with their dead!)

Perhaps it was balls they lacked, the careful poets—
Or a proper respect for the dead, being brutalized
By too much writing for the Sewanee Review and Co.
(Come down now, Don Gordon, there's the body of a man here no one
Is prepared to bury).
                                (No one prepared for John
Thomas: a woman behind every tree and the last tree
At Kodiak, a couple of years toward Christmas).

But no one comes down; only that corpse hung round
My neck by the circling bomber—a stiff in the cloud-high pastures
Of the lacklight, strange, permanent, feckless, enshrouding skies,
Prowling:

Fixed like the Hunter:
Fixed like the Bear:
In the cold house of the black starless North.

He did my dying for me.

                        To each his own place

According to his need:
According to his ability:
The dead:
In their crowded cities, the living
In their isolation.

5.

The armed children at their terrible play, John Thomas!
Into the gun-colored urine-smelling day, heroic,
The bombers go. The sad sacks and the wierd sods,
And the gay deceivers: cranked up into the loud sky
At the end of the immaculate chain of money.

                             The grieving day
Comes with its rains and ruins and across the bay and the drained
Downs where the fighter strip is, the guns go and the colored
Tracers mew and mow, for practice.
The planes loft up. The gunman children
 (The radar scope on the voting machine for fire power)
Like leaves in the cold heaven, flung forth in their bombers.

So the day comes.

                        And down to the hornacle mine
Under the arch of the tracers to dig for the faery gold.
In those days (wakening under the cold comforter snow,
Or awash above freezing water in our dug-down pyramidal tents,
Then wading into the fierce day, like mad frogs,
Amphibious); in those days (the wind
Exploding the tents out of the eight foot caves
Where, against the williwaws, we'd dug them in—
The whole thing blown inside out: the tent, the men,
The glowing, red-hot stove with its stolen high-octane fuel:
Blown into the empty lunar lots and the wide acres of the high North

Its lonely houses) ; In those Aleut days
(The dry-bones poets fussing over who owned the dead,
And the dead-ones in their high coffins singing around my ears—
Those windy bones) —From those days it's Cassidy I remember:
Who worked on the high steel in blue Manhattan
And built the top-most towers.

                                            Now on our island,
He was the shit-burner. He closed the slit-trench latrines
With a fiery oath.
                             When they had built permanent structures
And underlaid them with the halves of gasoline drums,
He took the drums out on the tundra in the full sight of God
And burned them clean.
                                Stinking, blackened, smelling
Like Ajax Ajakes, he brought home every night
(Into the swamped pryamidal, where, over two feet of water,
Drifting like Noah on the shifting Apocalypse
Of the speech of Preacher Noone, I read by the ginko light)
Brought home mortality, its small quotidian smell.

That was a hero come home! (The bombers swinging
Around his neck, the gunners blessing his craft
For dropping their load in comfort!) Him, who on the high and
                   windy
Sky of Manhattan had written his name in steel, sing now,
Oh poets!

But that's a hard man to get a line on.
Simple as a knife, with no more pretension than bread,
He worked his war like a bad job in hard times
When you couldn't afford to quit. He'd had bad jobs before
And had outwon them.
                               Now in a howl of sleet,
Or under the constant rain and the stinking flag of his guild,
He stood in his fire and burned the iron pots clean.

6.

"What a goddamned second-hand war!" says Harry Merer.
We are passing the fighter-strip boneyard in an eighty mile wind
With the horizontal rain going by us like buckshot.
The wrecked P40's glisten in the storm, their skins rattling
Under the slatting gusts.
"Like a goddamn Brooklyn junkyard,"
He says; and goes past the wreckage to the sand-bagged crash-tent
And Bob Kinkner and Charlie Wallant, and the long
Boredom.

         The war there was not one that could have been fought.
The Japs could have bought the island for two bottles of *sake*.
Still, it went on.
Cassidy stood in the wind, burning,
And we fought the weather: the fog solid around us
In a sixty-mile-an-hour gale, the sleet like gunshot
That ripped through the tent walls . . .

   (There is a corpse in the snow . . .
"It's dead, bury it," says the Captain.
There is a blue fox come into the chow line.
"Bless it," says Preacher Noone. "It's hungry; it's holy."
There's madman lives in my tent, got a two foot
      knife. "Shoot it,"
The Captain says, "It's alive; it fouls up my Morning Report."

So, another day rusts out in the windy light.

     *   *   *   *   *   *

Toward quarter-time in the afternoon, the sky breaks:
Its floor shifting and the tall walls falling off seaward;
A brief lifting: Like night's wake shied off by a rafter-raising
Gust of surreal noon.
               In that metaphysical space
(As between lover and lover, between Longfellow and Night)
The planes race out, race in: our own bombers and Jap
Fighters—the latter a little early, since the weather blows
     from their way—

All hurrying out and home) .

               The planes come in
From Adak, from Umnak—from as far as Cold Harbor the planes
Come out of the door of the weather and home at my window like bees.

(The mail has come in: people still know how to write.)

Then comes the counting of the sexual cost,
The great Vulvar Shift and the Gemination of Cunt:
 (The machine-gun's colored sperm is arching over the harbor
In a Blindman's 4th of July, where no man may speak,
And the hunting Hands—Oh Jesus Jason John Thomas—
In the high Oh Jerusalem fleece of the incoming fog,
Golden: in new-come sun: up to their balls in the sky)
Shot down at ten thousand miles by the blast of a Dear John.

Then the bombers:
Blown home on the squall line:
A jump behind buckshot:
Bad news:
At the end of the girls', fathers', shotguns'
12 gauge prejudice:
Blown out of the unkempt counties of the west unfriendly sky.
Those dead come home to the medics, frantic-megantic,
Dropped down the mail-slot of the early night
 (The mantic frail-quail and the fright-wigs, and the simple
Big-ass birds) . . .
               Burning . . .

                         Like Cassidy—
Burning: burning:

Then the calm evening—the one calm evening we all remembered:
And the dead planes come in, dropping like flung stones,
Like falling slow stars, burning, onto the flat preachments
Of the metalled runways hot gospel—a whirring blur of light
As of summer sparklers, and a huff and a puff of flame
Like a dream of Emma Goldman—the undropped bombs raining
Around our ears, the iron dung of those birds—and the dead

                              screaming

In their blazing cages.

We ran like rabbits down the dead flat road of their light
To snatch them home to the cold from the fiery cities of air,
Their sky-high blazing fox-holes and the smouldering houses
Of the zodiac of the dead.
                                    The medics came down
With their nine foot flutes, and the joy-pumps stuck in their arms,
To bind them home.
                                    We pulled them out of their rig,
Screaming, and gave them over to the mercy of the medical arm.

Then, in that one clear evening, the planes burned!
Fighters and bombers: P40s and 38s, B24s, 26s
Burning! Burning!
And the ammo burning, exploding, shot in the eye of heaven
The salmon-leaping tracers arching their backs to these stars—
Visible, newly, but shifted—and the whole for-once-bright evening
 (Old-fashioned 4th of July) under the changed constellations
Strange, in the high North.

_____carried them out.
And the meat-wagons took them away.
                                          Blue, green, yellow,
Their peculiar gear was burning across the night,
Those Roman Candles.
        There is a corpse in the snow . . .
        "It's dead, bury it," says the Captain.
        There is a blue fox come into the chow line.
        "Bless it," says Preacher Noone. "It's hungry; it's holy."
        There's a madman lives in my tent, got a two foot knife.
                "Shoot it,"
        The Captain says, "It's alive; it fouls up my Morning Report."

                                7.
                                          Then, Night.

Night, first of the high, great fog: blown down
From the vast Siberias and freezing unknown lands

Of the fierce bear and blue shy fox.

                                        Blown past our sleep

In the 90 mile wind, a shifting of space itself.

Night of the Army then: its paper snow: proper:
And its fog of number: cold: and its graceless mossy
Sleep, like wine in a stone ear.

                                        Night, too,

Of khaki: in the wet, cold dark, a claustrophobia
Of rancid clothing: implacable oppression of unchosen things,
A uniform irritation—though god knows
We dressed like bums, like pirates, in rain-clothing
Stolen from the Navy's house, its many mansions.
Still, heavy, heavy, was the wear of that alien skin.
Cold cave, rough womb, from which we could not be born,
It filed the dream to a vision of sharp light,
Some bright and burning beach and ourselves naked upon it—
The wild need to undress home to the Self.
A romanticism of light . . .

But now the dark comes down cold, like a wet beast
Dropped on the dreaming floor of a farther and other night,
Terrible.

                        Over the tundra the guns of the lost people,
The impatient ones, the midnight suicides,
Salute the war they have immoderately lost.

Fireworks in the rain! And the dark circus . . .
Now the night-crawlers and the water-walkers appear:
Those who go home by sea to the ten-foot line;
And then the ingenious: swallowers of razor blades,
Truck drivers with ten feet of hose, the inventors
Who have found something high enough or strong enough to hang on;
And the shy loonies who can fall off cliffs.

Oh night! Night! In the nine hundred countries of the endless war
How cold you come: and sane! John dear, dear
John Thomas what a burning in the snow there! In the blank,
In the year-long dark, in the night when Raisin Jack is your sergeant—

(The squads in the boondack outposts tip-toeing down to their stills,
And the gone medics—crazy—the needles thick in their skins,
A-dream in each others arms: the dying already dead
On their clean tables; and out in the storm the mad
Preachers calling curses into the rain) —

Oh holy night: how gone, how long you are!
Then was when I missed her—Marian—in the long missing.
(The long week-end I'd gone on) —missed her most
In that vast waste of the lost, the most abuse of the least,
In the burning and the freezing.

That kind of missing was like time running out of your arm
                    as blood will.
That was no cook-out in the Shack-up Mountains, but honest-to-god
Loss, as of too much blood, when the world turns grey as lichens
And you spin out left in the winter undersea light,
Pulled by the heart's torque.
                                        Pulled wrong way round
In the heavy night, with Time blowing past on the constant, high,
Wearing wind of that place.
                                        Not pain, not loss,
Not even guilt, but the slow seige of time:
        Time against money, for the ambitious
            Against muscle, for the worker
            Against Lady Jane, for John Thomas
            Against the Dream

                    *   *   *   *   *   *

Well, war is just unhappiness under a fancy name
With a lot of flags (and the fat farts of politicos
Up to their arms in the till) the continuation
Of confusion by other means, as Von Clausewitz said—
Anyway, that's how the night was: the rain whirling down
Like a blast of buckshot turned loose in an iron round-house
By anyone crazy enough.
                                        It was time running out,
The junky medics, night walking, stuck full of barbs
And the looney preachers, their ears ringing with gunshots

84

From the suicide farms, laying the Word out cold
In a thousand mile thick of the fog.

                                        And everyone yearning
For the Old Days and the Real War:
                    Soldier vs. civilian
                    Army vs. Navy
                    Men vs. Women
                    Rank and file vs. Secretary
                    Right vs. Wrong
                    Up vs. Down, Out vs. In, Least vs. Most.
                                        Oh holy night!

                              8.
Such were our losses: terrible and small:
   (_____They have heat-seeking missiles for that kind of jazz,
Thermotropic anonymous letters that explode at blood heat
And will blow you ass-ways just because you are warm . . .)
Part of the Engineer's great dream: a war without bandages.

It was through all this altruism that Cassidy moved,
Cloudy, in the oil and smoke of burning excrement,
In his fiery cloacal mask.
                                        Was run over, one day,
By an off-reservation aircraft.
                                        Nowhere, now, on the high
Steel will he mark on the sky that umber scratch
Where the arcing rivet ends.
                                        Gathered away
Toward the unknown stars, in the general drift toward Aries:
In the blanketing dark:
Salmony deadfall of the fishing Bear:
Outward:
His speed increasing to the speed of light and his mass infinite—
PUT THAT MAN DOWN, GOD!

                *   *   *   *   *   *

                                        Later . . .
And home then, the war ending . . .
The port: drifted two hundred miles to the south, the stars
Shifting in the permanent sky . . .
                                        Put me down

    sir.

XI

1.

Dream and despair; the journey around a wound . . .
Circularity again, with nothing laid true in a straight line
Nor square with the sailor star nor the fence of the north Forty
But turning, turning . . .
    Dakota, New York, Europe, Dakota again,
Los Angeles Frisco Dakota New York, Los Angeles
Turning and turning . . .
    Out-bound on the far night journey
As some long-chained animal, loosed, would pace his imagined cage
Turning, turning, I turned
Around the dead center of some unnamable loss:
Nowhere and nowhere . . .
    Like a man in the dark, searching
A vast wall for a door, through which he dreams his escape:
But he's on the outside . . .
    Or, like a man going round
And round some fog-bound lake, trying to find a crossing
 (The buried lake of the past in which he must drown)
Turning; turning and turning—
But never the direct voyage, the short journey toward the
     endless wound.

2.

They were fighting: soldiers, sailors, marines, civilians
As we came down the gangplank, or spilled out the door of a bar,
Fighting four sided, the whistles blowing, the cops and the
    MP's coming.
I tried to run; and the nightstick slugged me, and sang me home.

Then began the war that Patchen had foreseen:
"When the cops were there in sufficient numbers, they all blew their
    whistles together.

The fighting stopped, and everyone changed clothes—
(The civilians got off the worst because everyone wanted their duds)
Then the whistles were blown again, and the war ended:
There was five seconds of silence . . .
Everyone swapped sides, in accord with his clothing . . .
And the whistles blew once more and the fighting started again . . ."

New York then: picketing the Franco ship,
Walking around in circles in the end of an older war.
And Showboat Quinn, barefoot on 17th Street
In the early cold autumn, across from the CYO
(Where the local boys shot up the Puerto Rican newcomers) saying:
"What part of the fuckin' local pageant are *you?*"
Saying: "Money talks these days; stop whisperin' there in the dark;
"Get out in the stream and *sing!*"

And up the street, in Mac's pad, where he lay, great-chested,
Stuffed with the borrowed air of the pneumo shots,
The lads came: the activists, the hotshots and the live-o's
From the NMU, the ILA, the Teamsters and Electrical Workers
To pace up and down and curse.
                              Turning and turning
Fighting mainly each other.
                              Turning round, turning round
The massive and central grief, the great secret loss of the war:
The cantrip and singing circle dreaming against the cold.

And home then in the first black frost of the fierce and peaceful season—
High shine of the north drifting toward wilful Scorpio
In the waste of October light . . .
To a houseful of ghosts and a wild autumnal singing
Of the spilled seed and the lost hosts of the dead.
The rusty ports of the sun . . .
                              Turned, and returned, and alone,
And the moon in my pocket as thin as a lousy dime.
In the north Forty, the tractor has eaten the horse.
You can't hear the crying for the sound of the counting of money.

3.

We lay in the east room, Marian and I, in the cold October light,
Light of a hurrying moon blown past the few thin marestail clouds.
Downstairs my mother was singing her rosary over my brother's bones.
Under the North Sea somewhere the fishes were eating my friend,
And far in the woods-dark, on the coulee hills, toward the distant river,
Under the disturbing moon a coyote barked toward the Prime.
She, asking:
"Are you going then?"
"I don't know."
"Will you be gone long?"
"I don't know."
"Will you be back?"
"I don't
Know."

4.

Country full of strangers in their queer costumes . . .
And a hurrying fury clapperclawing their lack . . .
Bandits . . . murderers in medals holding hands in the catch-as-can dark
With the carking, harked-back-to, marked-down virgins of the stark
        little towns
Where, once, their paper histories dropped on the thin lawns
And rocking porches of the dead-eye dons and the home-grown
        dream-daddies
Now stiff with their war-won monies.

                              Bandits . . . gypsies—
Under the humped cloth of war . . .

                        Those sad children . . .
Older than headlines, under their khaki print.

And mad for money, those guys: for the lost pre-war
Land locked virgin and the homespun moss of her historical North
Forty.
        Aiee!
            Great God in a basket!
                      Those famous men

All green with their green-backed hope!

Country of strangers . . .
                       Myself strange, under the corroding moon,
And the cold charity of the first, thin, early, snow.

5.

Snow fell slight, pale filings of the icy sky, sifting
Fast into bare brown woods we went past in the thinned-out, down-fallen day,
Turning on the high hinge of the winter-come night.
                                 Some light still
Splintered on the height of the hueless corn . . .
                      ——————went through there—
And the pheasant leaped! Leaped out toward his death
In the feathery color of thunder!
                        Under the gun's black clap
Fell.
Enamel feathers; eye more round than his blood,
More jewelled, that stretched out neck with its ring of moonlight . . .

Red and Sorenson walk up out of the deepening gloom,
Through the leathery clatter of the thin corn that is shaking
               its winter rattles,
Still wearing their uniforms, talking of Saipan: of Marathon.
Red puts out his hand. "Too thin," he says
Feeling the bird's crop. "Farmers picked their corn
Too close this year. He's too thin. Leave him lay."

And that Fall the bandits went hunting—
Still in their uniforms, but getting too thick for 'em—
And shot up everything that could run fly or crawl.
Cleaned out the deer as slick as a whistle,
Bucks, does, the half-grown fauns and the yearlings—
Killed them with everything from buck-shot to Schmeissers and
               tommy guns;
Blew holes in them bigger than their own hard heads;
Hacked off a haunch and let them lay.
                      That Fall

Those gypsies in uniform drank all the wine of the province,
Down to the last corn-squeezins:
Ate all the food:
Screwed everything that could walk:
And ran off around break-up, just before spring work started,
Complaining of obscure hungers.

And myself, Tom Fool, ran with them: in a journey around my hat:
The cantrip circle dispersed:
Nothing to hold to:
No center there and no center in myself.
Leaving Marian, though we didn't know that till later,
Turning and turning.

Some ran toward money, and some toward hunger, and all were lost.
You have seen the bones in bank-vaults, or on glass cases over the bars
Among the foreign money, where Custer once fought
And the great golden nude slumbered above the whiskey.
Do those bones live? Do they sing still in the whirling
Dust on the Grandfather stair where first my loves were singing?

They sing still; and are still; in the grandfather dark.

6.

It was that dark I entered, blown toward no certain shore,
Turning and turning.
                              Past the Indian graves and the river,
Past the north Forty, past Dakota, New York, Villefranche,
Past love, past work, past any plan, past hope
Past sex, past whiskey, past defeat, past
The bottom of the interior night and that antipodeon great beast
(Whose charity is to devour) past common sense
And solidarity —
Oh journey — Oh journies — around the unnamable years
And circumvention of joy . . .

And come at last to the condominium of monsters:
Ulan Bator of the Outside:

Fantastic go-downs and submerged kralls
Of the underground man.
And swam there in the sea-light of alcohol and unspeakable loss,
In that parade of freaks:

> A bandage comes by wearing a man
> A walking eye with a cunt grown on its pupil
> The Porcupine Man with his hide stuck full of syringes
> The Lady Built Backwards
> Geeks, ploot, quim, loogans and hooples,
> Liz's and queens and
> Pathics with the rough trade of the quarter,
> The benny-workers and the Monday-men,
> Wino chenangos,
> Lumpers, humpers and keester-bumpers,
> The Monkey with the Man on his Back,
> High-graders, God-hoppers, mission-stiffs, marks and
> sharpies,
> Punks and meat-heads *Apackapus Americanus*
> Drifters, queers, losers; the underground men
> Hung on the pukey weather of the skidrow street.

And continual wind of money, that blows the birds through the clocks,
That plucks a cold harp inside the bellies of horses;
In those days: a blizzard of continual bones
Under the stony sky of the counting heart.
In those days—blood of the dead freezing in blind eyes.
House of smoke, hour bitter as knives,
And the avalanche, cooling its fevers, on the second floor of your tomb.

Nightmare, nightmare; despair; dream; and despair.

7.

It was down there,
Past the milestones of my tombs and the singing bones of my true loves
I come there:
Drifting:
In the high march and dead set of the night,
On the most direct road to my death—
Most careless there—

I come into the Old Dominion, the true, breathing, holy, Dark.
There, old bird on the branch of the lost midnight,
The Dark closed and clothed me, and the pushed, furious beast
That burned and bit in my side lay down to sleep.
Hushed at last.

Then I saw the bones go singing—
Like stars or fireflies—
And came to the laughter:
The Holy Joke of myself in that blizzard of dark and light:
To Laughter:
Laughter of light and dark and the Holy Joke of that real world,
And the great open secret that we all know and forget.
Samadhi. Satori.

Then the great night and its canting monsters turned holy around me.
Laughably holy.
And that lank gentleman, the esthete snake, came by to bite me,
And the littlest scared mad dog of a crazy world,
And I gave them my heel to kiss—
In my sudden pride:
In my quick ridiculous love:
In my wholeness and holiness:
In solidarity and indifference:
In the wild, indifferent joy which is man's true estate.

Love and hunger: solidarity and indifference—
So I ended my journey to the enduring wound,
In the holy and laughing night with the stars drifting
Indifferent;
And myself indifferently drifting
Past the randy Goat and the Water-carrier,
Past Easter, and the high Feast of the Fools,
In the thin rain of the time.

XII

1.

All changed; the world turned holy; and nothing changed:
There being nothing to change or needing change; and everything
Still to change and be changed . . .

Now . . .
            Past Solstice . . .
                           The infrequent rain
Of a cold, unseasonal season . . .
                       My neglected, arrogant garden
Lifts in the night its indifferent gold and green:
Fuschia with its Greek fighters and Dutch girls;
And the freckled small tunnels of Foxglove which the bee drifts;
Yellow Iris, bronze Day Lily, Lupin, Larkspur, Linaria
Bend in the chill, thin rain: infrequent: past Easter and the Feast
Of Fools.
               Night now:
                            First neighbor's dog
Frets at the ghost of a moon.
                         Mourning like a lost ship
A diesel hoots and harks in the railroad yards, past the river;
And the dead come home, riding the blinds, at last
Crossing the dark mountains after the months of snow.

2.

Strange season now, nothing but wars and the sound of money
And the hills alive with crazy men and deserters . . .
_____and past Capistrano, where the road cuts down to the ocean,
Past oil fields where the pumps like herds of great insects,
Prayerful, bow and dahven:
                          We head south, to the Border,
To export the Revolution, taking Mac into Mexico.

After the Immigration ordered his self-deportation.

1955 that was: on a cold afternoon:
Autumn dropping its metal in the blue wound of the weather
And the papers full of news from the scientists
Who were dreaming of wars without blood, of blowing us clean
               out of history
Without even the need for a bandaid.

                                   Past Pedro
Where Mac had been organizer: past the strikes, past the Thirties
Past the Baltimore Soviet, past the Bremen where Mac
Had cut down the Nazi flag—

For the exile it is always ten degrees colder beyond the border.
Southward, to Ensenada,
To the cold sea and the confusion of foreign speech
I took him.
"Goodby Tom Fool," he says
Last of my fathers.

3.

"When the fix is equal, justice must prevail" . . .
Blue violence of the eye, that lends its shape to the world
Fixes no proper image for the times.
The Committee comes by with its masked performers
To fire you out of your job, but that's expected.
Money breeds in the dark—expected.
Weeping and loss—expected.
_____What was hard to imagine were the do-it-yourself kits
With 4 nails and a hammer and a patented folding cross,
And all the poets, green in the brown hills, running . . .

I needed a ward for the Now, to nail its hide to the barn . . .
There is one of Lubner's paintings—people among the rocks
Refugees, a Madonna with a curious witless smile,
A mystery.
                 Also a great gentle horse, and a man with an odd
Figured shirt and several women in black,
And there ought to be (but there isn't) a bird-cage with, in it—
What?

A tame star, perhaps?

Working in the animal foundry, I puzzle toward it.
Schwartz is burning the horns of an Ibex, perhaps—
Product of his dark fancy—and I daydream through the sound
Of the wood saw and the drift of the golden poisonous dust:
And see Mac standing—Mac or Cal—with Maggie his wife
And a scatter of Mexican kids by the ocean's cold confusion—
An image of exile.

I turn away then
Unforgetting
Seeing a little piece of the old true unregenerate dark
Extruded into the afternoon classical light—
A little Contra-Terrene matter among the pure shit of the poets—
The world's inescapable evil that we must eat and sing.

And turn away then
From the shop, from the sea,
Toward the desert of the world, the wild garden,
With my politics: to be with the victims and fighters.
Turn North, toward the dry river, to journey in sunlight
Beyond the sea's conventions and the winter's iron and ice.

4.

Blesséd, blesséd
            Oh blesséd
Blesséd be changing day and night and the old far-ranging
Starry signs of the loved, continual, surprising seasons;
Blesséd be dark and light, blesséd be freezing and burning,
Blesséd be the gold fur of the He-sun and the moons-down shine
            of the great
Bold, changing, Woman queening the wild night-sky;
Blesséd be the metric green confusion of the crowding, cold, estranging and inconstant sea;
Blesséd be the stay-at-home land, the rocking mountains under the loose loud sky;
Blesséd be speech and silence;
Blesséd be the blood hung like a bell in my body's branching tree;
Blesséd be dung and honey;
Blesséd be the strong key of my sex in her womb, by cock and by

                    cunt blesséd
The electric bird of desire, trapped in the locked-room mysteries of country charm;
Blesséd be my writing hand and arm and the black lands of my secret heart.

Blesséd be the birds of the high forest hung on a wing of song;
Blesséd be the long sin of the snake and his fangs blessed;
Blesséd be the fishing bear in his shine and fury;
Blesséd be flower and weed: shoot, spike, rhizome, raceme, sepal and petal;
The blued-out wildlings; metallic, green marsh-hiders shy; high-climbers, low-rooters.
Beast, bird, tree, stone, star: blesséd, blesséd.

And blesséd be friends and comrades:
Blesséd be Rolfe in his dark house and the hearts of friends.
Blesséd, by the loud continuous sea: Naomi.
Blesséd on their mountains under the enshrouding shine of the spent stars' light:
                                                    Don and Charlie:
With their wives, children, heir and assigns.
Blesséd, blesséd
In the waste lots and the burning cities of man's estate,
Fishers by still streams, hunters on the hard hills, singers, dreamers and makers:
Blesséd be all friends
With their wives, husbands, lovers, sons, daughters, heirs and assigns
Forever.
Blesséd be the fighters:
The unknown angry man at the end of the idiot-stick with his dream of freedom;
Jawsmiths and soap boxers, gandy-dancers setting the high iron
Toward the ultimate Medicine Hat: blesséd, blesséd.
Blesséd the agitator: whose touch makes the dead walk;
Blesséd the organizer: who discovers the strength of wounds;
Blesséd all fighters.

Blesséd be my loves: in the wreckage of morning light,
In the high moon-farms, in the horny hot night of the dry, gone summers,
In the heat of lust and thunder of the noon sheets—
Blesséd be flesh and voice, blesséd forever;
Blesséd thy belly and legs;
Blesséd be thy woman's warmth in this human winter.

Blesséd, blesséd

                                        Oh blesséd
Blesséd be Marian,
All ways the honey flesh of this girl with light on her shoulder
Oh blesséd, blesséd!

And blesséd now be all children:
Hunters come through the space warp, waking
Into their unmade world under the sign of our outlaw fire;
Blesséd their hopes and confusions;
Blesséd their deeps and darks
Their friends and lovers, heirs and assigns forever.

And blesséd, blesséd, blesséd, blesséd
Be my wife and love, and her body's being:
Green song of the double-meaning sea;
Tree of my dreamless bird, unsleeping quarry of seamless
Light; feathery river of the sensùal continent, unseasonal rain
Under the riven sky of my dry thunderstruck night-side heart
Unending lightning . . . . .
                                        Oh blesséd!
And blesséd myself and myselves . . .
Turning homeward . . .
                        under the waking shapes of the rain . . . . .
Blesséd.

                                5.
Now, toward midnight, the rain ends.
The flowers bow and whisper and hush;
                                        the clouds break
And the great blazing constellations rush up out of the dark
To hang in the flaming North . . . .
Arcturus, the Bear, the Hunter
Burning . . . . .

Now, though the Furies come, my furious Beast,
I have heard the Laughter,
And I go forward from catastrophe to disaster
Indifferent: singing:

My great ghosts and the Zodiac of my dead
Swing round my dream.

Star-shine steady over this house where I sit writing this down—
2714 Marsh Street—
                    Drifting toward Gemini . . .
Night, pure crystal,
           coils in my ear like
                          song . . .

                        Los Angeles, 1955

PART TWO

Everything or nothing! All of us or none.

Bertolt Brecht

...luck, chance, and talent are of no avail, and the man who wishes to wrest something from Destiny must venture into that perilous margin-country where the norms of Society count for nothing and the demands and guarantees of the group are no longer valid. He must travel to where the police have no sway, to the limits of physical resistance and the far point of physical and moral suffering. Once in this unpredictable borderland a man may vanish, never to return; or he may acquire for himself, from among the immense repertory of unexploited forces which surrounds any well-regulated society, some personal provision of power; and when this happens an otherwise inflexible social order may be cancelled in favour of the man who has risked everything . . . Society as a whole teaches its members that their only hope of salvation, within the established order, lies in an absurd and despairing attempt to get free of that order.

Claude Levi-Strauss

Don't give your right name! No, no, no!

Fats Waller

I

1.

_____coils in my ear like song. . .

                                   the dawn wind riding
Out of the black sea, knocks at my shutters. Cockcrow.
Before cockcrow: the iron poet striding over
This village where the horses sleep on the roofs, where now a lone
Rooster rasps the beak of his song on the crumbling tiles.

Skyros.
   In the false light before sun-up.
I wait while the breeze,
Or a ghost, calls at the shutters.
                             Beyond the window the wild
Salt north 40 of wind and water, the loud, galloping
White maned mustangs of the cold ungovernable sea. . .

Honeysuckle, lavender, oleander, osiers, olive trees, acanthus—
All leafsplit, seedshaken, buckling under the drive
Of the living orient red wind
                         constant abrasive
North Dakota
             is everywhere.
                   This town where Theseus sleeps on his hill—
Dead like Crazy Horse.
             This poverty.
                 This dialectic of money—
Dakota is everywhere.
             A condition.
                   And I am only a device of memory
To call forth into this Present the flowering dead and the living
To enter the labyrinth and blaze the trail for the enduring journey
Toward the rounddance and commune of light. . .
                         to dive through the night of rock

(In which the statues of heroes sleep) beyond history to Origin
To build that Legend where all journies are one
                                        where Identity
Exists
        where speech becomes song

                *   *   *   *   *   *

                        First bird sound now. . . . . .
This morning Lambrakis overthrew the government in ghostridden Athens
Having that power of the dead out of which all life proceeds. . .
Genya smiles in her sleep. The arch of her foot is darkened
With the salt of the ancient sea and the oil of a bad century. . .
The light sharpens.
                The wind lifts.
                        The iron poet
Strides out of the night and the instant world begins
Outside this window.
                World where the rebels fall under
The Socratic tricycles of NATO gangsters, are plugged in the heart
By intercontinental ballistic musical moments mechanical
Pianos loaded with the short-fuse scrap iron of Missouri waltzes, guided
Missiles of presidential rocking chairs timed to explode on contact. . .
Texas fraternal barbeques: "Bring your own nigger or be one".

(And, of a mountain of wild thyme, its thunderous honey).
The sea builds instantaneous lace which rots in full motion —
One-second half-life — just beyond this window.
                                        Full light.
Cicadas.
        A donkey brays on the citadel.
                                The world,
                                        perfect,
And terrible.
        Sun in Gemini.
                        New moon at summer solstice
Perfect.

* * * * * *

     All changed and nothing changed and all to be changed.
I want the enduring rock, but the rock shifts, the wind
Lifts, Hell's always handy, you may enter the labyrinth anywhere
Beyond the window.
                Where now the first fisherman goes out:
To the mother sea, to mine for the small fish and the big—
The hours and minutes of her circular heart— to dig in the turquoise
Galleries of her tides and diamondstudded lobsters with their eyes of anthracite. . .
Where his partner, the Hanged Man
                     strangled in nets of poverty. . .
                               last night. . .

Last night. This morning. The rock and the wind.
                 North Dakota *is*

Everywhere.

               2.
"_____seems like it was right here somewhere. . .
                   place where you git out—
Hey there, resurrection man! ghost haunter, crazy damn poet,
What you do now kid?"
          (Voices from sleep, from death, from
The demoniacal dream called living.)
               —I'm here to bring you
Into the light of speech, the insurrectionary powwow
Of the dynamite men and the doomsday spielers, to sing you
Home from the night.
       Night of America.
           Gather you
At my millionwatt spiritlamp, to lead you forward forever, to conquer
The past and the future. . .

* * * * * *

105

                  "Well just a doggoned minute now,
Whilst I gits my possibles sack, my soogans, my—"

                         —Heavy,
Heavy the weight of these choice souls on my sun-barked shoulder, heavy
The dark of the deep rock of the past, the coded legend
In the discontinuous strata where every voice exists—
Simultaneous recall: stone where the living flower leaps
From the angry bones of precambrian dead.

                     Heavy the weight
Of Jim, of Jack, of my father, of Cal, of Lambrakis, Grimau,
Hiroshima, Cuba, Jackson. . .
                 heavy the weight of my dead
And the terrible weight of the living.

               *   *   *   *   *   *

                 "It's dark down here, man—
This slippery black—can't keep my footin'—like climbin'
A greased pole, man—"
              And always, as I go forward,
And older I hear behind me, intolerable, the ghostlight footsteps—
Jimmy perhaps; or Jack; my father; Cal; Mac maybe—
The dead and the living—and to turn back toward them—that loved past—
Would be to offer my body to the loud crows and the crass
Lewd jackals of time and money, the academy of dream-scalpers, the mad
Congressional Committees on Fame, to be put on a criss-cross for not wearing
The alien smell of the death they love
                   —they'd cram my bonnet
With a Presidential sonnet: they'd find my corpse worth stuffing
With the strontium 90 of tame praise, the First Lady to flay me
For mounting in the glass house of an official anthology. . .
                       catafalques
Of bourgeois sensibility
          —Box A to Box Z. . .
                  And my body to suffer
(As my soul) dismemberment. . .
             transmemberment. . .

                                        my head
                                                singing
                                                        go down

The dark river. . .
                        necessary —
                                Not to turn back.

                        *   *   *   *   *   *

"_____and seems like it was right here someplace — place you git out. . ."
"Stick beans in your nose and you cain't smell honey." (Peets talking)
"Ain't no grabirons a man can lay hand to. *I tell you it's* DARK
DOWN HERE MAN!
                        slippery dark
                                        can't see
                                                I tell you it's hell — "

We must walk up out of this dark using what charms we have.
Hell's everywhere, this only seems like hell, take my hand,
It is only required to open your eyes —
                                        see
                                                there's
The land as it was
                        these poor
                                the Indian graveyard
                                                the coulee
The quaking aspens Genya and I planted last spring
At the old farmhouse.
                        Unchanged and changed.
                                                I tell you millions
Are moving.
                Pentagon marchers!
                                Prague May Day locomotives
With flowers in their teeth!
                                And now the red ball is hammering in —
Spot an empty! Grab an armful of rods!

                                        I'll take you
In the final direction. . .
                        Only:
                                        open your eyes. . .
But it's hard, hard, man.
                        I'm standing *here,* naked
As a studhorse in a rhubarb patch
                                        Waiting
                                                waiting
                                                        and here —
Around me
                trouble built for small boys and crazy men!
For my purpose (as I keep saying) is nothing less
Than the interpositioning of a fence of ghosts (living and dead)
Between the atomic sewing machines of bourgeois ideology
(Net where we strangle) and the Naked Man of the Round Dance. . .
"To perform instantaneous insurrectionary lobotomies for removing
The man-eating spinning wheels from the heads of our native capitalists."
To elaborate the iconic dynamite of the authentic class struggle
In other words to change the world
                                        — Nothing less.
                                                It's hard and I'm
Scared. . .

                        *   *   *   *   *   *

        The beginning is right here:
                                ON THIS PAGE.
Outside the window are all the materials.
                                But I am waiting
For the colored stone. . .
                                for the ghosts to come out of the night. . .

And now the village sleeps.
                        A heavy static
                                golden
Like the honey of lovesick buzz-saws clots in the steepy light

And the tall and aureate oak of the august noonhigh sun
Crumbles.
        That pollen.
                Seeding the air. . .
                        The cicadas (tzinzaras)
Are machining the sunlight in their chattering mills
                          kind of morse code
With a terrible signal-to-noise ratio — is it information
Comes through all that clatter or a mere random conformity
To a known Code?
        Minimax
            bobbery
                palaver
                    — you can reduce shortfall
Only so much — finally. . .
                it is necessary to act.
                      Even
When the information is incomplete. . .
                  — That's all right:
I'll cut for sign — and don't leave the gate open
                    I'll
Catch my own snipes.
           The village is *not* asleep, it is only
Siesta. . .

        A poor fisherman hanged in a net
Puts all heaven in a sweat. . .
              The ratio of signal
To noise improves. I read you loud and clear. Over.

 "— get out in the stream and *sing*.
              It's a branch assignment,
                    a job
For the revolutionary fraction in the Amalgamated Union of False Magicians,
Kind of boring, from within. . . "

                    Insurrectionary
                                ancestral voices. . .
                                            —coming now—
Ghosts wreathed with invincible wampum—
                                "Hey buddy
What you doing there in the dark?"
                                —How should I know?
                                            What I'm doing
Ain't nobody
            nowhere
                    never
                        done before.

II

1.

Fictional breakfasts, feasts of illusionary light!

"Poo ine

O dromos sto horyo where is the lonesome road
To the village where is it the hydroaeroplano leaves
For Buenos Aires?"

I'll cut for sign. . .

mark of the blazed tree

Where I left the note and the colored stone in the hopeful intervals
Between cyclones and water spouts, while the firing squads
Were taking a five minute break. . .

"—was right here, someplace. . .

___place where I left it. . ."

Patience.

I am the light. I'm

Wearing my blazer. . .

Begun before Easter in the holy sign

Of the Fish.

Dakota.

The farm house. . .

—but before that. . .

*   *   *   *   *   *

Ten years—doing time in detention camps of the spirit,
Grounded in Twin Plague Harbor with comrades Flotsom & Jetsom:
Wreckage of sunken boats becalmed in the Horse Latitudes
Windless soul's doldrums LosAngeles AsiaMinor of the intellect
Exile.

I arrived in the form of a dream, the dream formed
Journey begun in love and hunger, Dakota, the Old
Dominion of darkness. . .

from labor

ignitable books

111

                                                        unsettled
Terms of a murderous century
                                        dynamite
                                                the eternal bourgeois
Verities of poverty and money—to voyage forth toward the light. . .

Got there by way of War and His cousin Personal Misery.
And of that journey and time and the records thereof kept
As of books written   logs   tallies   maps   manifestoes
As of resolutions past or not passed in aforementioned intervals
Between stampedes   shipwrecks   log jams   battles with hostiles
Catatonic inventions   hellsfire   attacks of personal and spurious
Revelation—
            Tokens:
                        stone
                            marked tree
                                        immortal
Blazonings. . .

                        2.
Windless city built on decaying granite, loose ends
Without end or beginning and nothing to tie to, city down hill
From the high mania of our nineteenth century destiny—what's loose
Rolls there, what's square slides, anything not tied down
Flies in. . .
            kind of petrified shitstorm.
                                    Retractable
Swimming pools.
                    Cancer farms.
                                    Whale dung
At the bottom of the American night refugees tourists elastic
Watches. . .

        Vertical city shaped like an inverse hell:
At three feet above tide mark, at hunger line, are the lachrymose
Cities of the plain weeping in the sulphurous smog; Annaheim:

South Gate (smell of decaying dreams in the dead air)
San Pedro Land's End. . .
                              —where the color of labor is dark—
(Though sweat's all one color) around Barrio No Tengo,
Among the Nogotnicks of the Metaphysical Mattress Factory, where the money is made.

And the second level: among the sons of the petty B's—
The first monkey on the back of South Gate, labor—at the ten
Thousand a year line (though still in the smog's sweet stench)
The Johnny Come Earlies of the middling class:
                                             morality
                                                   fink-size
Automatic rosaries with live Christs on them and cross-shaped purloined
Two-car swimming pools full of holy water. . .
                              From here God goes
Uphill.
        Level to level.
                      Instant escalation of money—up!
To Cadillac country.

                      Here, in the hush of the long green,
The leather priests of the hieratic dollar enclave to bless
The lush-working washing machines of the Protestant Ethic ecumenical
Laundries: to steam the blood from the bills—O see O see how
Labor His Sublime Negation streams in the firmament!
Don't does all here; whatever is mean is clean.

And to sweep their mountain tops clear of coyotes and currency climbers
They have karate-smokers and judo-hypes, the junkies of pain,
Cooking up small boys' fantasies of mental muscles, distilling
A magic of gouged eyes, secret holds, charm
Of the high school girls demi-virginity and secret weapon
Of the pudenda pachucas (takes a short hair type
For a long hair joke) power queers; socially-acceptable sadists—
Will tear your arm off for a nickel and sell it back for a dime.

And these but the stammering simulacra of the Rand Corpse wise men—
Scientists who have lost the good of the intellect, mechanico-humanoids
Antiseptically manufactured by the Faustian humunculus process.
And how they dream in their gelded towers these demi-men!
(Singing of overkill, kriegspiel, singing of blindfold chess—
Sort of ainaleckshul rasslin matches to sharpen their fantasies
Like a scout knife.)
                Necrophiles.
                              Money protectors. . .
—They dream of a future founded on fire, on a planned coincidence
Of time and sulphur. . .
                      Heraclitian eschatology. . .

And over it all, god's face,
                        or perhaps a baboon's ass
In the shape of an IBM beams toward another war.
One is to labor, two is to rob, three is to kill.
Executive
        legislative
                judiciary. . .
                          —muggery, buggery, and thuggery
All Los Angeles
            America
                is divided into three parts.

                *   *   *   *   *   *

"If you can't screw 'em—join 'em", Peets says. "They come here
Answerin' the *Call.*"
                And it may be.
                      The distant horn sounding. . .

They heard it first perhaps in the faded, dreaming polemical
Grandfather cadence: how this one caught the old bear
Belted for winter swimming the cold lake; how the last deer,
Antlers in mossy felt, shot down in the aspen scantlings
Fell: as the final take of the long march west; how the light failed

While the flights of wild geese crossed on their high arch of darkness
Calling.
        The land failed them; or else they failed the land.

And turned westward their canvas-covered argosies
Freighted with dreams: the Daniel Boones of the last myth
Toward free land and free labor, the commune and round dance
Journeying. . .
        But a myth's not as good as a mile.
                Came to the echoing
Horns of Disneyland, faintly blowing; to the jockeys of nightmare
The dream scalpers and the installment purchase blue blood banks
Of the Never-Never Plan.
        The dream had ended but they didn't know it —
Rootless at Hollywood and Vine slumbering in rented shoes.
And still *there*!
        —chained to the chariots of Scythian kings. . .

Times change.
        The wind shifts.
                There are countries with no
Immediate future worth having.

                This is the windless
City.
    Dead air.
        Dynamite, dynamite
                dynamite. . .
Time and change. . .
        the rock and the wind. . .
                —and *still* stand there—
At the end of the line: "one jump away from salt water". . .
Turn
    round!
        (*Turn round the wagons here,* saith the poet.)

```
*    *    *    *    *    *
```

"God *damn* that motherin' Hairyclitoris principle!
Hell's hell! It's *some'eres!* It's *this neck a' the woods!*"
(Mr. Epitaph Peets bawling on the none-o'clock jump.)
"Everything's happle at Hairy Apple!

                             write me here —

Casa Salsipuede
    Nem Mukodik utca
        Quartier Sauvequipeutville
            Texicola
                New Dada
                    Unida Anada"

3.

Phase change around midnight. By the light of the underground moon
That wake I ride through this range of loss and these wide loose acres
Of stony total damnation in the white unparalleled lost
City. . .

        Many nights, ghosting these shores in the shifting moonshine,
I read the weather-signs of the spirit and the spoor of the sour times:
The citizens wrapped like mummies in their coats of poisoned sleep,
The dreamers, crazed, in their thousands, nailed to a tree of wine,
And written on the bold brow of the filthy unbending sky,
And sung among imperfect strangers, chanted in studio back lots,
Among three-way Annies and gay caballeros at home on all ranges,
Or shouted in top-secret factories where they make inflatable breasts,
Sung by the glove-faced masters of money with the sex of knives,
By the million grandmothers drying like cod, like anti-cod, like blind
Robins in the smoky terraces of Pasadena, rung out
On the gold-plated telephones in bankers graves at Forest Lawn,
In the unbalanced books of sleep where the natives dream on credit —
Sung out in every language, alive in the sky as fire,
Is the Word:
        the little word:

                    the word of their love:
                                        to die.

                    *   *   *   *   *   *

"Traveller under the street lamp, I am farther from home than you."
Not so, old poet, Dreamy Don Gordon. No farther than I was:
Among the gigantico-necrosaurs, who misread size
For vitality, wheeling dervishes mistaking speed for movement—
These records put down between flash floods and forest fires:
(My duty to keep the tally-book: me: ring-tailed roarer
And blue blazer—I'm wearing my blazer) this sacred page
The burning bush and rune stone emblem of Plague Harbor
Necessary document   .
                    laughter out of the dark
                                        this sign
Of a time when the wood was in love with fire, the fire with water. . .

Not all of it like that either, no place being perfect in death.
Myself there to make a winter count and to mine my bread.
And others like me:
                    mavericks in lonesome canyons, singing
Into the desert. . .
                    Bone-laced shining silence faced us. . .
—But sang there!
                    "Making a little coffee against the cold"—
(Alvaro showed me.)
                    Inventing again the commune and round
Song gathering the Crazy Horse Resistance and Marsh St. Irregulars,
Building the Ramshackle Socialist Victory Party (RSVP)
And Union of Poets.
                    Bad times.
                            The Revolution
Decaying as fast as the American Dream—whose isotope lead
Bloomed in the nightsticks of the company cops.
                                        And we offered our bodies:
On the Endless Picket Line of the Last of the Live-O Americans

                            117

For the Rosenbergs, murdered by Truman and Ironhead Eisenhower—
For all the lost strikes sold out by the labor fakers
Of Business Unionism Reuther Meany Social Plutocracy;
For Communists jailed or on the run in the violent darkness;
For the Negro sold again and again in slavetrade Washington—
And lent them our bodies there, giving our blood to that other
Dream. . .
       It still lives somewhere. . .
              accept these tokens. . .

Lived there.
       And every morning down to the hornacle mine,
To the vast dream foundries and mythical money go-downs
Of the city of death. (And always with Comrades Flotsam and Jetsom!)
Reading the wish to die in translatable shirts of autochthons,
Blacklisted by trade unions we once had suffered to build,
Shot down under a bust of Plato by HUAC and AAUP.

Outlaws
    system beaters
        we held to the hard road
(While Establishment Poets, like bats, in caves with color T.V.
Slept upside down in clusters: a ripe fruited scrambling of ass holes.)
But it's a hard system to beat: working under the hat
On the half-pay offered to outlaws by the fellow-travellers of money:

And time runs fast on a poor man's watch.
         Marsh St. eroded.
Dry wells. . .
       But I still remember the flowers and Cisco singing
Alive
    and the flowering names of that commune of laughter and light
Those I have named and the others—flowers of a bitter season—
They'll know who I mean. . .
        And I worked there.
           I went to work in the dark.

I made poems out of wreckage, terror, poverty, love.
Survived.
            But times end.
                        My wife was looking uphill
Toward the Gadget Tree (was last seen crossing over the smog line
Approaching an outpost of sports cars).
                                    We came at last to a house
With more windows than money: and written over the door —
(In fire I think) — NO DREAMS IN THIS HOUSE!
                                        But my dream begins
Three dreams to the left. . .

                *   *   *   *   *   *

                        Well — money talks. It's hard
To say "love" loud enough in all that mechanical clamor
And perhaps the commune must fail in the filth of the American night —
Fail for a time. . .
                But all time is redeemed by the single man —
Who remembers and resurrects.
                        And I remember.
                                    I keep
The winter count.
                And will remember and hold you always although
Fortuna, her heavy wheel, go over these hearts and houses.

Marsh Street. . .
                blowing into the universe. . .
                                    winds rising
                                            change.

                        4.
Twice, now, I've gone back there, like a part-time ghost
To the wrecked houses and the blasted courts of the dream
Where the freeway is pushing through.
                        Snake country now.
                                    Rats-run —
Bearable, bearable —

Winos retreat and the midnight newfound lands—
Bearable, perfectly bearable—
Of hungering rich lovers under the troubling moon
Their condominium;
                    bowery close; momentary
                                        kingdom—
Wild country of love that exists before the concrete
Is poured:
            squatters there.
                        That's all
O.K. with me.

*   *   *   *   *   *

First time I went back there—about an age ago come Monday—
I went hunting flowers: flowering bushes, flowering shrubs, flowering
Years-grown-over gardens: what was transportable.
What was transportable had been taken long away.
Among the detritus, rock-slides, confessions, emotional morrains—
Along the dream plazas and the alleys of the gone moon—
Some stragglers and wildlings: poppy, sorrel, nightblooming
Nothing.
            And found finally my own garden—where it had been—
A pissed-upon landscape now, full of joy-riding
Beer cans and condoms all love's used up these days
Empty wine bottles wrappers for synthetic bread

*   *   *   *   *   *

Larkspur, lupin, lavender, lantana, linaria, lovage.
And the foxglove's furry thimble and the tiny chime of fushia
All gone.
            The children's rooms have a roof of Nothing
And walls of the four wild winds.
                                And, in the rooms of the night,
The true foundation and threshing floor of love,
Are the scars of the rocking bed, and, on certain nights, the moon.

Unending landscape. . .
                              dry. . .
                                        blind robins. . .

                    *   *   *   *   *   *

Blind Robins, Blind Robins — Fisherman, do you take Blind Robins
In the stony trough of the dry Los Angeles river?
No charmed run of ale wives or swarming of holy mackerel
From the pentecostal cloud chambers of the sex-charged sea, no
Leaping salmon on the light-embroidered ladders of eternal redemption?
Damnation of blind robins. . .
                              bacalao. . .
                                        dried cod, is that,
Is that all you take on your dead-rod green-fishing Jonah,
Poor boy, mad clean crazy lad I pulled once from this river in spate it is not
Bearable.

                    *   *   *   *   *   *

Well, wait, then.
                    Observe.
                              Sky-writing pigeons, their
Blue unanswerable documents of flight, their
Unearthly attachments.
                    Observe:
                              these last poor flowers,
                                        Their light-shot promises,
That immortality, green-signature of their blood. . .

Now, instantly, the concrete comes: the freeway leaps over the dead
River and this once now twice-green moment into the astonished
Suburbs of the imaginary city petrified
Megalopolitan grief   homesteads of lost angels   anguish. . .

On this day nothing rises from the dead, the river
Dying, the dry flowers going under the mechanic stone. . .

                              121

                                                    Sirs!
Archaeologists! what will you find at that level of ancient light?
Poverty destroyed sweet hearts and houses once before Progress His Engines
Put down a final roof on the wild kitchens of that older
Order.
            These lovers long are fled into the storm.
The river is dry.
                  It is finally.
                              completely
Bearable

                              5.
____All funeral wreaths must wilt around my neck
In time.
                  From that place they ship all bodies east.
And eastward I went
                        turning
                              crossing the dark mountains
In the months of snow
                        turning
                              Los Angeles, San Fran, New York
And return.
                  Sustained only by a thin gruel of moonlight
And the knowledge that all was perfection outside my prison of skin.

And perfect there also, although it seemed for a time
That the villain mathematics had sown in the dreaming soul's dark
A sick fancy of number: but there's no number higher
Than One.
            All number drowns and dances
                                    in still light
                                          the great
Aleph of Satori. . .

                  New York, then. . .
                              granite island, mighty

                              122

Rock where the spirit gleams and groans in the prison stone:
Held there in black entrapments: soul's Harlems: the steamy
Enchantments of lack and luck: the lonely crucifixions
In the ten thousand endless streets of the megalopolitan dark. . .

And did you come there in summer, tobaggoning in the slow sheets
Of earliest love; come there to work your secret name
On the frozen time of a wall; and did you come there riding
The tall and handsome horse whose name's catastrophe?
I came there
        I loved
            I rebelled with others
                    I shed my blood
With theirs and we bled a dream alive in the cold streets.
And returned there: after the wars and the years: and colder those iron
Plateaus, and older that dream, and the rapid walls are rusting:
Immortal slogans
        fading
            that we wrote in fire out of need. . .
Out of need and the generous wish — for love and hunger's the whole

Burden of song. . .

            And went down there — after years and wars and whores
And loaves and fishes: the double-dyed miracles pulled off by Generals
Motors and Moonshine (those gents' act: to starve you while stuffed
With the jawbreaker candy of continual war: the silent American:
Mounted
        automated members of the Hellfire Club
                    Zombies).
And the talking walls had forgotten our names, down at the Front,
Where the seamen fought and the longshoremen struck the great ships
In the War of the Poor.
        And the NMU has moved to the deep south
(Below Fourteenth) and built them a kind of a Moorish whorehouse
For a union hall. And the lads who built that union are gone.

Dead. Deep sixed. Read out of the books. Expelled. Members
Of the Ninety-Nine year Club. . .

                                    "Business unionism!" says Showboat
(Quinn). "It certainly do hit the spot with the bosses!
Backdoor charters and sweetheart contracts — sell out the workers
And become a by-god proletarian statesmen like Sweet Walter.
Takes a liberal kind of a stiff to make labor-fakin' a *pure* art."
Had swallowed the anchor, that one.

                                        And many thousands gone
Who were once the conscience and pride of the cold streets of the workers;
Dissolved in numbers is that second Aleph, the Order of Militants,
And the workers defenseless: corralled in the death camps of money
Stoned in a rented dream frozen into a mask
Of false consciousness. . .

                    lip-zipped

                                    the eyes padlocked the ears
Fully transistorized

                    — living a life not their own.
Lost. . .

Still, in the still streets, sometimes, I see them moving —
Sleepwalkers in nightmare, drifting the battlefields of a war
They don't even know is happening —

                                    O blessed at the end of a nightstick,
Put to bed in the dark in a painting by Jackson Rauschenberg,
Machined to fit the print in a rack 'n' gawk juke box, stomped
By a runaway herd of Genet fagots, shot full of holes
By the bounty hunters of Mad Avenue, brains drawn off
By the oak-borers of Ivy League schools' mistletoe masters.
Everything's been Los Angelized. . .

                                    Alone, now, in the street,
What sign, what blazed tree, what burning lightning of the radical Word
Shall write their names on the wall break down that mind-framed dark?

Northern lights in winter; in summer the eccentric stairs
The firefly climbs. . .

                    But where is the steering star
                                              where is
The Plow? the Wheel?
                        Made this song in a bad time. . .
No revolutionary song now, no revolutionary
Party
        sell out
                    false consciousness
                                    yet I *will*
Sing
        for these poor
                    for the victory still to come
RSVP

Stone city. . .
                    and the dumb struck dim wonders
(Crow voice, hoar head, pig mug)
Citizens of Want County as the Bowery spreads its diseases—
Contemporaries. . .
                            An age of darkness has entered that stone
In a few years between wars.   The past holds,
Like a sad dream trapped in granite: what foot can slip free what trail
Blaze in that night-rock where the starry travellers search?

I hear them knock at the far doors of the night I see
Through the haze of marble those shadowy forms. . .
                                    comrades. . .
                                              I'll sing you
Out of the prison stone, I'll pick the lock of your night. . .

But lonesome song, for a fact.   History's been put into deep-freeze
In libraries and museums. . .
                            those limestone bowers its prisons. . .
But still the wind blows and the stone shakes in the night
Sometimes. . .
                a shrill singing wakes in the granite matrix:

Music of bone flutes, a skeleton harp the wind
Thumbs and fondles. . .
                              skull-trumpets. . .
                                            voices under the ice. . .
The song I hear them singing is the Miseries and the Terrors of New York. . .

The misery of morning when the moneyclock turns loose its five loud lions
(The lion of the landlord, the lion of bread, the lion of a lone girl
Dying in Cheyenne, and the twin lions of loss and age.)
Terror of morning late dreams like clouds stuffed
With eagles of scrap-iron: sagging over the slow fires
Of anxious beds: those peat-bogs that once held hands with the lightning.

The misery of six o'clock and the nightshift oozing like ghosts
Sidereal ectoplasm through hell holes in pavements: a scandal
Of blind birds swelling the clogged sleeve of the dead-lighted
Dayside. . .
              a host burning
                            a nation of smoke. . .

Terror of the time clock mechanical salaams low pressure systems
Blowing out of the nightbound heart's high Saharas,
A muezzin of blood blazing in a cage built out of doves. . .
Terror of the noonday bullhorn pulling its string of sound
Out of the lunch box: time where the tides rage off Hatteras
And the drowned locomotives roll like dream monsters slow in the grip
Of the clashing vast deep: and their bells chime: and the whistle rust
Lights submarine tunnels toward dead harbors, sounding far stations
Closed forever. . .
                        retired at sea
                                    their circular shoes
Still

    Terror of the quitting hour, the air full of skinning knives
And the damp buffalo falling through the scaly tenement walls.

Thin-fit lives: tamped matrimonial gunpowder, ancestral pistols.

And the terrors and miseries of the arc of darkness extending past midnight:
Charismatic lightning of alcohol dead in its chapel of glass,
The harping dream-song in the round ditches of revolving roads
Silent. The last ship sinking on the sea of a wounded brow—
All terror and misery present now in the loud and dying
Parish past midnight—a thousand fast mustangs freezing in juke box
Ice, the little shelters built out of temporal wine
Blowing away in the wind the night-bound death wranglers
Stumbling into the day
                              wait.
                      For the angel.
                                  Wait.

In New York at five past money, they cut the cord of his sleep.
In New York at the ten past money they mortgaged the road of his tongue,
Slipped past the great church of song and planted a century of silence
On the round hearts' hill where the clocktower the cock and the moon
Sang.
        At a quarter past money in New York a star of ashes
Falls in Harlem and on Avenue C strychnine condenses
In the secret cloisters of the artichoke.
                                  At half past money in New York
They seed the clouds of his sleep with explosive carbon of psalms,
Mottoes, prayers in fortran, credit cards.
                                  At a quarter to money
In New York the universal blood pump is stuffed full of stock quotations:
And at Money all time is money.
                        False consciousness.
                                  Bobbery.

Meanwhile, of course
                —wait for the angel. . .
                                  Meanwhile of course. . .

6.

Wait. Wait. The long waiting like the long running:
In the cold. In la noche oscura darknight of Kelvin. Of Godot.

On the avenue of C, which Christ led into this slaughter house,
A wintry dynamite of absentee landlords, misplaced herrenheit,
Explodes the compesinos into the East River ice.
Tall walls fall.
        Slow.
                Aristocratic
Exfoliation.
           But *that's* the work of ice, not wind. . .

And came down there in a bad time – if there's any other
Time on that lost way.
                Time when the moon is full
Of abandoned beds, fissioned by sexual centigrade, lofted
Out of the black apostle streets where the C note sings.

Waited there on the cold plain with Charlie and Mimi
For the wind to shift, granite to wear, our stony history
Turn a bright page: waited for nightmare to open. . .
(All those years in detention camps of the spirit, waiting!)
Meanwhile, of course, smuggling a few guns to the distant
And distancing counties – the ones reached only by laser and Lazarus –
To the truly outside Johns.
                Meanwhile occasional *de*rail
Of the soft express: the one turned round at the Finland Station
By the plastic professors, by two-car agitators and labor-fakers
Who were bundling Lenin back into Switzerland.
                        But all that
With dreamy dynamite: the slow fuse made from my blood
And gism.
           I waited that year for the light to turn
Blue.

For the dream.
                              —'cause I'm a fast dreamer, a dream
                                                        champ.

"—Times I been there myself (Mac speaking). You got to play it
By ass, like a country whore in a ten dollar house. There's some
Couldn't pump piss from a ten gallon hat with a sandpoint.
                                                    I *been*

On *that* corner.
                    Been give up for left, lost *and* dead;
Been busted, disgusted and not to be trusted; been struck by lightning
Hellsfire and congress; seduced by playgirls: half female and half
Playtex; signed petitions: ALL POWER TO THE PEOPLES'
NEUROSIS; found some dark glasses and become a humanist;
Holden 5 kings—man had six bullets. It don't
Hump me none to stand in this cold. I was born *here*. . .
Seegaseega."

            Seegaseega.
                        Take it easy
You've got the moon in your pocket and the dark fur of the night
To warm.
                And a charm of pot croons in a far safe
Where Dorothy sings.
                        Where Genya will come.
                                        (But later.)
                                                While the rifles—
Bill Epton's, are oiled but sleeping in Harlem's frost and fire. . .

But, hard.
                Granite matrix of false consciousness.
                                            No kite
Nor lyre to fly over the fatal deep of the lost
Farfallen city.
                Dead anticyclones.

Anti-historical
Highs and hang-ups slumber in the tranced inhuman stone. . .

—and Charlie kept me alive there:
                              Humbolt:
                                        the warm current.
—Making a little coffee against the cold—it was Alvaro
Taught us all.
                    And daily he went out in the New York night
(To the hornacle mine) with Mimi.
                                        Each dark they wrote the names.
(Lent him my blazer sometimes: to see in the spider-colored
I-spy light.)
                    In those days the revolution had come down
To a voting machine in East Asshole Georgia, an off-color
Jerk or joke in the Let-My-People au Go Go night
Court club.
                    And the Catholic liberals taking instruction
From the stiff theses of a Bald Twin while El Roy Bones
Is preparing his nation's house: ie to yell *Mother fucker*
In the Mies Van der Rohe jakes of the ancient Anglo-Saxon death.

And I'm for it, of course, you can't put down the dead nor the grave
And bravely living.
                    And some of my best friends are dead.
                                                  And black.
And dead for unfashionable things the bourgeois just don't dig:
Be they white *or* black.
                    But I mean blacks' not *all* black, you come *right* down to
It.
    NOTHING'S all *that* perfect.
                              At the congress of the color blind
I put up the communist banner my father signed and sang:
LABOR IN A BLACK SKIN CAN'T BE FREE WHILE WHITE SKIN LABOR IS IN CHAINS!
Or, otherwise:
"Everything or nothing— all of us or none:
We better all be swingen when the wagon come."

130

*   *   *   *   *   *

Wait for the Angel.
                  S A Q U A S O H U H:
                                the blue star
Far off, but coming.
                  Invisible yet.
                        Announcing the Fifth
World
      (Hopi prophecy)
                    world we shall enter soon:
When the Blue Star kachina, its manifested spirit,
Shall dance the *kisonvi* for the first time.
                          In still light
Wait.

"But it's cold here!"
                Hush.
                  I'll take you as far as the river;
But no one may dream home the Revolution today though we offer
Our daily blood, nor form from the hurt black need
The all-color red world of the poor, nor in the soviet
Of students transform this might; nor alcohol compound
Manifestos; nor pot set straight a sleepy rifle's dream.

Still we must try.
                S A Q U A S O H U H.
                            Far off: the blue
Star.
      The Fifth World. Coming.
                      Now, try:
Necessary, first, the Blue Star kachina to dance the *kisonvi*;
Necessary that the *kapani* at the crown of the head must be
Kept open always.
                Loosen your wigs.
                    I go to the far
Country

to the sacred butte and the empty land

I'll make

The kachina. . .

7.

Alcohol is the labyrinth, ganja the curved arrow, but labor
Is the low high-road to our common heaven.

(make the kachina.)

    Time to return to the grand labor of the resurrection man the
Blue blazer. . .

    Windless Los Angeles built on decaying granite
And windy Manhattan entombed in its granite sleep these impotent
Contradictions. . .

    What holds nothing and what imprisons
All ways:
    locked-room mysteries of tradition or history blown
In the cold and bone-choked wind to the farthest ends of the night.

It was time then to be going from that place to another.
Lunacy of cities, idiocy of the villages—turned away
Toward a marriage of rock and wind, toward stony lonesome,

the high

Country.
    To do a little coyote.
    To make the kachina. . .

Goin' to Dakota to throw the hoolyann. . .

    "Beyond Chicago
The true snow begins"
    Fitzgerald said it.
    Went there
Sixty years into the wrong century, carrying

The Medicine Bundle.
                   (It was Genya showed me.)
                                     To make
The kachina. . .

                *   *   *   *   *   *

Far.
      Dark.
            Cold.
                 (I am a journey toward a distant
And perfect wound)
                   —got there in the blazing winter night
(January showing its teeth like a black wolf in the north,
And the blank farmbuildings fenced with ancient sleep)
                                  —to the stark
And empty boyhood house where the journey first began. . .
—to search there, in the weather-making highs, in the continental sleep
For the lost sign, blazed tree, for the hidden place
The century went wrong: to find in the Wobbly footprint Cal's
Country. . .
             —and sat there
                    in those first nights:
                             waiting
(Genya, the ransom of cities, and all my past, sleeping
And the ghosts loud round my light)
                    Waiting.
                           Southbound, the coulee
Carries its freight of moonlight toward the fox-brightened river breaks.
All time condenses here. Dakota is everywhere. The world
Is always outside this window: Now: a blaze of January
Heat: the coyote: the cicadas of Skyrian snow—all *here*
Now or later.
             (The poem is merely what happens
                               now
On this page. . .)

Night here.
                    The breathing dark.
Cave of sleep.
              I enter.
                    Descending is ascending.
                                   Go down
Past the stone decades and the bitter states of the anguished and enchanted salt
Toward my dead.
                    A static of hatching crystals ticks in the rock
Like a clock of ice.
                    The dead swim through the night-stone, homing
Into my side.
              Come now
                    my darlings
                              my dear ones
                                        begin
The difficult rising.
              I'll help you.
                         Slip your foot free of the stone—
I'll take you as far as the river.
                    Sing now.
                         We'll make the kachina.

III

1.

Begun before Easter. . .

                  the snow rasps on the porch, the cicadas

Rust in the long sealight

                 — and the poem going on forever

Forever

          — coyote calling his last late-winter song

In Skyros' caroling heat   Dakota   high   lonesome

Twilight.

        The owl circling. . .

                    — over the windfall trees. . .

*   *   *   *   *   *

Out of imperfect confusion to argue a purer chaos. . .

Bare-handed   start there: and my hands are

Barer than most at best: and after ten years on the blacklist

Barest. Embarassed and bare-assed, like my master: go into the woods:

With an ax. High thinking and low chopping keeps baby's

Ass warm.

        Bad case of the Gotta-No-Gots.

Start *there,* then.

*   *   *   *   *   *

        So, next day, go out:

Sunny midweek morning no more than 40 below;

Take the doublebitt ax, the crosscut and bucksaw and go

(Trailing an oily stink in the stun-breath cold — kerosene:

To work the rust off the blades).

                Enter the ancient woodlot

My grandfather planned and planted and prayed from the virgin soil.

Stand alone there, at the first tree: and strike!

Old cock of Nowhere crowing: alive in the winter light!
Tree of rusty stone: it kicks out sparks like flint—
Like wintry fireflies in the deadfall gloom they arc down, dying!
Elzevir edition meteors, pigwidgeon-planets, dandyprats—
Almost I heard them sizzle, burning out in the snow!

And now a great hush: the universe halts: holding its breath
For the death of those infant worlds and the great shout of this my labor
Done for love only.
                    Halts for a moment.
                                        Then the great bush
Of the silence unfurls in a fury of snow cursed out of a towering
Ash tree by a lout of a blasphemous Jay.
                                        He knows
My name.
          All of 'em.
                      And the little world awakes, scolding:
"The bronco's back on the range! The lunatic's in the trees,
Chopping wood for the purest hell of it, wouldn't you know!"
And the crows come by to stone me, and the Jay is filing his tongue
Like the deaf man tuning a buzz saw, and around in the ark-fat farms
They turn up their thermostats. . .
                                    And one blow does all this,
One man cutting wood for fun, for the blaze of his own work!

In joy.
        That does it.
                      Rockefeller revolves like a goose on a spit
In his whited sepulcher
                        a Texaco station goes down with all hands
Off Venezuela. . .
                   This ax, comrades, has blasphemed against fuel oil. . .

                    *   *   *   *   *   *

First crack out of the box and the tree takes a bite of my ax!

                              136

Check that.

        Fact. There's a dent in the bit.

                    The cheek

Sinister.

      Examine:

           —a stone grown under the hide of the tree!
From the long-gone summer cyclone that laid these deadfalls down:
This marriage of wood and stone, the tree taking into its system
This outer and alien order.

           I lift my ax and go on.

All through the brilliant morning the woods rang.

                    But slower—
Toward noon.

        My muscles like wet newspapers—and ones morever
Containing archaic disasters and the deaths of long lost friends. . .
The cold

      pure crystal.

             The dead calm air like glass. And a chiming
Of thin and distant voices from the milesaway red-roofed farms
Carrying perfect over the bonewhite blazing, the blank blinding
Perfection of the empty fields.

          Train sounds. Far.

                And near
My animals-in-law, the red squirrels, their furry coal
Aglow in the flocculent cloud-shifting drifts of the newdown petalperfect
Platonic snow.

          Across in the feed-lot my cousin's cattle—
The high-haunched Holsteins and ground-gripper Herefords drop their dung
And the steam, like the crooked smoke   the god's love, rises
Shining.

      High passing through.

             The great wheel of the winds
Still.

Blue
        eye of weather
                Sun
                        Smile.

Cottonwood. Ash. Oak. Chokecherry. Box Elder. Elm:
Trees of the wind-down deadfalls I mined that sovereign day
For the circular light of their dusty hearts, the ringed roads
Where the riding lust of the highwayman's sun in summers by
(Lifelightyears away) buried his august and aureate warmth.

Cottonwood. Box Elder. Chokecherry. Elm. Ash. Oak—
And not like that other winter we got wood up from the river:
The cantrip and singing circle, last commune and round song,
The bunched cooperative labor of poor stiffs in the cold.
All dead now: that kind of working. Only
The trees the same: cottonwood; chokecherry; elm; ash;
Oak and box elder.
                Every man on his own.
                                It's here
Someplace
        all went wrong.
                        For work alone is play
Or slavery.
        Went wrong somewhere.
                                I'll find it for you—I'll blaze
That tree. . .
            Cottonwood, chokecherry, box elder, oak, ash, elm. . .
I rip them out of the drifts and clap them flat on the block.

                *   *   *   *   *   *

Working alone is play
                is a way back
                        (maybe)
To something lost. . .
                I enter the world of the dead, the stormdowned

Deadfalls: I mine for my darling these stovelengths of buried light this
Ancestral warmth. . .
                              And home in the early dusk. The cold
Steel-sharp and still.
                              Full moon pale in the deadfall.
                                                            First stars
Burn:
        The winter dark is setting its clock toward Spring its
Blazing integers of ancient light:
                                    smoulder and sing.
And the feathery gears and pinions of the continental highs and lows
Mesh; turn; wind.
                        The helix of terrestrial winds
Drifts and shifts: slow: a new season works forward. . .

History is the labyrinth, Art is the curved arrow, but Labor
Is the gunstraight line to our common heaven.
                                    (Play or slavery. . .)

You expect?
            Nothing.
                    Hope?
                            Nothing.
                                    What do you want?
Nothing.
        All's well.
                    Inside the prison of skin. . .

Now into the woods in the starry dusk goes the hustling winter
Crow: the dark's collateral and raucous eclipse of light—one bar
Of late-winter-early night: late, late he goes home.

Glass   falls   now   winds   rising
                                change

Working alone is play or slavery.

                        And working with others?

Slavery or play.

              Or the holy roundsong of labor danced

Out of love and need. World outside the invention of surplus

Value.

        Prewar and westerly, that.

                  But once upon a distant time. . .

          *   *   *   *   *   *

"Doublebarrelled shitepoke sheepcroakes, swillbelly like a poison pup!"

Packy O'Sullivan down from the wilds of the Irish Bronx

Speaking.

          Of the hemisemidemifascist leadman, the pipeshop plague.

"Corkonian motherjumper — steal slop from a blind sow:

He would. Put him in rubber boots and kick his royal

Ass so hard that he'd bounce so high they'd have to shoot him

To stave off starvation!"

                Ah! Uses of anti-aircraft

In Federal Drydock & Shipyard. O

                   in the merry months of war!

(Kearney New Jersey.)

             Now out, like a weasel down-hole he rushes,

Like a Bantu beater rousting a thicket for a pride of lions,

To a jackstraw deadfall and lumberjacks dread of a log jam:

The stacked unwelded pipes' blind cuckoos' nest.

— Leaps (as at insult) with a chain-fall, to quarry there

(Out of confusion) the ghost-grey galvo and the dung-dark iron.

Comes in. Swinging on the chain-fall chainsend his pick of the heap

Some Dead-Sea-monster-shape unarticulated: built up, like pride,

In the (almost) infinitely reticulated blueprint mind.

(Got to be mind somewhere if you're building a ship.) He drags

It: to the wheel of the welding table; lifts his catch
And turns the wheel.
                        I hit an arc, building a loop,
And bead the joint with bubbling, steely, vitriolic ovals
In Palmer Method.
                        Under my mask the fierce destroying light
Softens is softened.
                        I look out of my Platonic cave into
Hellsfire: electrico-magnetico-mechanico-metallico seventh
Circle. But soft.
                        Turning the wheel in the ancient way.

And over and around me the cacodemons are building arches
Of purest noise.
                        Ancestral loup-garoux and banshee assholes
(With attendant clurichaunes, deevs, afreets, dwergers, bogies—
Each hell-hurrying at the top of his stick to create the Domdaniel
And instant Malebolge, the Broad Church of Blast). *Now Hear This:*
Here: first the spitting arc under the poisonous
Smoke I build: at the end of my line the welding machine
Barks   whines   groans: the chainfall is rattling and grinding
Like judgment day on a dental farm: and the demon benders
Squeeze out of their Torquemada-machines the bass moans
Of the teninch pipe.
                        Ah, Dy, bach—there's organ music
Would last a Welsh choir till Maundy Thursday or Hell-come-Sunday.

A little nightmusic now: add in the anti-boss cursing,
And rehearsed squeals from the whoring cunts in the wild world of the yard—
And a distant keen of money from the cost-plus counting machines.
Morgan's Allgotnick's Bank.
                        They rinse out exhausted condoms:
A double sawbuck!
                        Or Johnny come early:
                                        a fast five.

"After the war we'll get them," Packy says.

　　　　　　　　　　　　　　He dives
Into the iron bosque to bring me another knickknack.
The other helpers swarm into it. Pipes are swinging
As the chain-falls move on their rails in.

　　　　　　　　　　　　　Moment of peace.
The welders stand and stretch, their masks lifted, palefaced.
Then the iron comes onto the stands; the helpers turn to the wheels;
The welders, like horses in fly-time, jerk their heads and the masks
Drop. Now demon-dark they sit at the wheeled turntables,
Strike their arcs and light spurts out of their hands.

　　　　　　　　　　　　　　　　"After
The war we'll shake the bosses' tree till the money rains
Like crab-apples. Faith, we'll put them under the ground."
After the war.
　　　　　　Faith.
　　　　　　　　Left wing of the IRA
That one.
　　　　　Still dreaming of dynamite.
　　　　　　　　　　　　I nod my head,
The mask falls.
　　　　　　Our little smokes rise into roaring heaven.

Graveyard shift in the pipe-welding shop at Federal Ship.
Half way through is the lunch break.
　　　　　　　　　　　The machines die.
　　　　　　　　　　　　　　　A stunned
Uneasy silence falls on the vast infernal yards.
One by one on the Ways the arcs of the deck-top welders
Sputter out. The burners' fires and furies are quenched.
The guns of the riveters hush their yammer.
　　　　　　　　　　　　　Peace is growing.
Like a midnight mysterious flower, its tendrils enter the beams
And bones.

But only a moment: this is the waking hour
For the cost-plus featherbedders who come forth from their dewy bowers,
The camouflaged tax-endowed nests where they sleep the long shifts through.
The hour of the numbers man and the bookie, the hour of the cost-plus
Whore (if you're padding a payroll and have two men for one job
You might as well have some women as well). Eagerly they come
(Like dollar-a-year merchant-patriots to the Washington swill-barrel
Where the blood-money contracts are made)   come out now to offer
Their All-American service: a little three o'clock jump
For the heroical war-workers weary. Historical commerce.

The peace ends.
                    The machines roar into life.
                                        The malignant
Arcs of the welders sizzle across the darkness.
                                        The yard
Groans and curses and shakes, tormented, as if to tear loose
From the anchoring stone and mount toward heaven on its anguished song.

                *   *   *   *   *   *

They are sending me down to the Ways where I don't want to go.
                                                    But I go.

Under the ghost-walking gantries sky-hung leaning out
Of the high dark.
                    Past the rolling-mill's raven and red fire.
Past the hosting riggers trolling the winch lines down out of darkness
And talking a load of steel away into the night.
A conversation of learned hands.
                            I walk under
The signs and signatures of lawful fire—great constellations
Flare and burn and hiss where the black hulks rise:
Galaxies flash and fall. Zodiacs of angry forms
Fill and fail, form and reform, shine and flame out.

Now a thin drizzle softens the light.

                    The welders
In cloudy aureoles, the burners in auras and saints' halos
Move.
              Dangerous rain.
                         On bad nights the air
Thickens with falling metal: dropped tools, rivets, men:
A general Fall, everything descending.
                                   I go into the ship.
Descend.
          Lower.
                    And lower.
                              Down to the inner bottoms.

                                                  Now
I am inside the whale.
                    Voices sound.
                                   Far.
A world away.
                    But I am umbilical: tied to a war
By electric cable, by a blower to breathe out the poisonous fumes
From the iron I weld.
                    In this strange cave with branching tunnels
(A claustrophobe's hell) the ship's lowest intestine (diseased:
With odd growths of pipe and wire, gobs and gobbets
Monstrous, necrotic) I crawl; hearing, sometimes (not knowing
Whether far or near) some worm and comrade in a brother shaft
Working along in the dark like me.
                              (And some to die there,
And they to bring cutting torches to burn you clear of the ship.)
Worked there (waiting for light and the new day, end
Of the long night shift) and at every turning:
                                        immortal
Blazonings:
          Kilroy was here.
                    Or Clem's mark:
                                   the inspector

Had been there before me.
                              In his sign I went on.
And so into the dark on that blazed trail
Night long.
                    And not so lonely with the fellow worker gone
Into the dark ahead.
                              Finally: another morning.

                         *   *   *   *   *   *

Morning when the eagle screams: payday. End of the long
Nightweek.
                    By the curbside dog-wagons the workers stand and wait
Till the pay office opens. The welders, easy to spot, swilling
Their quarts of milk to damp the burn in their bowels.
                                                   (It's poison—
Welding-smoke of galvanized iron puts fire in your belly, O
Poets!)
              The office opens.
                              We sweat the line
                                        Count it
And run.

Strange world of the early morning the night shift
Enters. . .
              Mysterious
                              Because we come in from the opposite side
Of time.
              In the newcome sun the island over the river
Is translated fresh from the darkness and born again in our glance
Out of another dimension where all night long it swam
Discrete, tenuous, the parts drifting away from each other
Like a drowned ship on the seafloor breaking apart. . .
And the dayside men come drugged, their heads milky with poison
Of sleep while their veins are throbbing still: the mechanical pianos
Of dreams, their heavy music. . .
                              darkening. . .

145

And we to them
Distant perhaps: the daze of the work still on us and the grey
Of the nightside world. . .
                              O tanist, twin, O ancient
Brightness: accept us: strangers: come home out of the dark!

                    *   *   *   *   *   *

At Paddy-the-Pig's then stand and drink the payday cup.
Where the last flyblown freelunch like the haunch of a hairy mammoth
In time's cold aspic sickens: but holds from a gentler day
The antique welcome.
                    "Slan leat!" says Packy.
                                        Peers out
Of his internal Siberia (that's brightened by the eyes of wolves
Only). "Down all bosses! After the war we'll get them!"

Ay. But the war got us first. Got the working class
By its own fat ass: screwed by the metal whore of gadgets,
Bought off and fobbed off by the Mad Avenue sou-soul fashioner's
Bobbery and palaver of false consciousness: doing the sacramental
Till-death-do-us-part on the Never-Never Plan of Death-by Installment,
In the Holy Layaway Order of Resurrection: meditating
On the four last things: as: psychiatristsportscarswimmingpoolstatus.
Mercenary eschatology!
                    Here's a blaze surely
Where we went down the wrong trail hellbent. And a long way home
—Father in heaven and if not where and if not why not?
—Let in a little air! Can't breathe for the galvo!

Still, hard to blame them.
                         They came to it pluperfectpisspoor;
The Gottanogotnicks from Barrio No Tengo and the raunchy and rancid
Haywire-and-gunny-sack shanties of a cold and hungry time:
Out of the iron thirties and into the Garden of War profiteers.
Once it was: *All of us or no one!* Now it's *I'll get mine!*

146

People who were never warm before napalm, who learned to eat
By biting spikes, who were bedless before strontium 90
Hollowed their bones: the first war victims. . .
                                      — in cost-plush cars.

Bought up.
          Corrupted:
                      their dream was that the war should
Go on forever.
                  And it hasn't stopped yet: one war or another. . .
And the guilt comes there:
                            sold to the stony generals
Their sons go forth to die for dad's merrie Oldsmobile:
(Kind of Layaway Plan)
                      —to die in a great blaze.
Of money.
          Blaze they went wrong by.
                                      And here's the first
Sellout from which the country is a quarter century sick.

                  *   *   *   *   *   *

Bugles!
        Parade!
                The mad generals are coming.
                                      They are leading a captive,
A twoheaded falloutmade monster, disarmed and dearmed by napalm,
Orphaned by Navy, unhoused by Air Force, tortured by Army —
In closest collaboration with syphilitic fascists and quislings
From the boy's own home country — (which the generals cannot
Pronounce).
                And after the enemy passes the patriots come:
Bespectacled professorial mass murders all ivy grown:
The gentle swingers and makers of minds from Mad Ave:
A farmer carrying a pet pig: a pop artist
Palpitant on a field argent (escutcheon of a home grown

Brass-ass millionairess: money from arms)

             Hats off!

A labor statesman in Brooks Brothers harness, with cadillac, passes

(The light a nimbus on the ring in his nose):

               and now the workers —

(Blood to the elbows) out of the arms plants to cheer a mortal

Victory.

    And afterwards came the rest.

              A nation in chains

Called freedom.

       A nation of murders — O say, can you see

Yourself among them?

         You?

            Hypocrite

              lecteur

                patriot

      * * * * * *

But Packy's not among them anyway: crossed to another quarter

One morning we left the ways where we launched the great ships;

(The holes in the whistles alone weighed seventeen pounds)

               turned

To the whys and wherefores and whores and hang ups of that other war

Where fascism seemed deadlier and easier to fight — but wasn't.

— Never came back, that one.

        But most of that time I remember

Kilroy — immortal spelunker! Man I never met

(Or joke perhaps — ghost-joke: ubiquitous as god His Name

On every wall later) who in the dark night

Of the innerbottoms cramped hell crawling worked always ahead

To scrawl his fame in a rebel joke or slogan, to point

To the work that had to be done.

          Where's Kilroy now?

             Turned

From one dark to another or lost in the war's fast shuffle?

In the underground lightning of a deadman's bones I see him

Writing his slogans still on the closed door of the world.
We see them sometimes yet. . .
                              And that too
                                             is a blaze. . .

                         3.
Megalomaniacalpseudomniestheticalisticalistical!
Lobster for breakfast! McJoseph: Of the Cadillac of many colors!
War-built millionaire and all-round retired Revolutionaire:
Too far left for this world and not right for the next.

Man with four projects and the first: never to die.
Second: to fabricate a glass heart: in case his own
Softened — what? — into mere mortality.
                              Third: to build
A little something to go with the first man to the moon —
(Middle initial V: for Vicarious). Finally: four:
To set up a small savoir-faire-farm in the wilds west
Of Beverly Hells: in Brentwood: to become culture-faker-in-chief
To Lost Angels to gar a crasis of replication on all
Fronts.
         Had arranged with god about point one and bought
Factories (didn't trust god) for points three and four and got —
God — another god — only knows how — a Brentwood newspaper.
The Weekly Nuisance.
                   Throwaway.
                              Carried the price of beans
At all supermarkets: pictures of the mayor's daughter: homey
Jazz to flutter shopkeepers and keep the ads flattering in.
The idea was to turn this garbagewrapper into
A glorious garland of gallant invention and hip prose foundry,
To spread a rich compost of culture in Hell-Beyond-Beverly —
Where on Sunday the kiddy-car lawnmowers are roaring like lions in suburbia!

Puerperous parturient publisher! All-Begetting Renaissance Man!
(And a good man enough, though a little forgetful at times
That he dealt with mortals: a god's weakness perhaps: or absent —

Mindedness induced by a rare virus *spondulix sempervirens* —
Had been bitten by money as a small boy and carried the marks
On his soul, poor man.

        Gave rise to strange behavior, sometimes:
As, instance: to go forth finned with a bloody big
Can of oxygen on his back to the great green mother
Sea: a parting of waters; to drop down the blue
Fathoms, salt; to sink in the tide's groin, cold;
To come to some drowned sea-cave or the littered table of the sea's
Underside; to sit there, mopant like a sad case of the sulks:
Counting his money.

        Wheeze and thump of his mask.

                Curious
Fish.

    Still, a good man for all that, the Metawampum Kid,
Wheeze.

    Thump. Thump. Money under the sea.

And myself to edit that paper having come by blacklist degrees
To the bottom: dropped out of the labor market as unsafe
To a government at wars ie the cold, the Korean, the Pretend
(Against Russia) the Holy (against Satanic citizens the likes of
Myself).

        And so came there to the capital of Paranoia
Brentwood.

        To the savage citizens — the last of the 49ers —
Who had come by to beat gold out of the rocks:
To pan for the wily megabuck from downgrade up-hill film stars
Their zodiacal houses and constellated-many-mansions secure
On the fast decaying granite of L.A.'s collapsible hills

But the declination of filmstars never approaches the smog line.
And the citizens camping in their hip-kisch shops among their mouldering
Go-to-hell-or-Paris ballgowns gay and their gimcrack quack
Art (their pisspots fur-lined and fey and their handworked French
Ticklers) got small smell of that money: only the spoor
To make them squall like wolves on a winter night, ravenous.

So they saw me as a claim jumper or bold bandido
Come with my willow wand to dowse for astral gold.
To cross the village square was to tread the thin crust
Of the petty-B inferno hate-hot.
                                        One middling class
ESPer and my body would swing for the carrion crow
On the ornate fake 90's lamppost: seditious scribe pro-
Thanatory perilous!

                        And J.J. McJoseph my jingalo johnny gave
Me — as co-conspirators and penance for sins — helpers:
Two (three would have been enough and one too many).
Primero: Coca (a demi-liz para-alcoholic) and Mister
Twister (O Prester John!) the master pressman (consultant
To the three kings of Azusa and Cucamongas royal Raz) —
Debile meathead and absquatulant horse's ass!
                                        Ten times
Around the corner and over the wall: quasiresident
Of the loud funnyfarms. Fat flatulent and phthisic.
                                        And Coca
The perfect bitch to lead him a dog's life.
                                        (And *her* ploy
To sink the paper and buy it up cheap with the help of her pressman
Whom she pressed often on the muezzin-screaming leather of the editorial couch.

So she screwed them both at once: the printer in his sanctum pandemonium
And McJoseph (J.J.) at long distance: he having answered the call
Of culture in upper Italy. (And J.J. helping her out
By non-payment of press runs to drive down the twistering prices
Of Mister T.
            O Trinity Unholy!
                        O Kilroy where
Art thou!)

                        So Friday all sleepless dark we put to bed

Our Cosmic Courier.
                    Nightlong.
                                        Last on the list of Mister
Eponymous Twister as deadbeat rep and walking delegate
Of transcontinental conman and carpetbagger J.J. McJoe.

I might be out at the stone, the presses thumping around me.
(And the office sofa thumping Cacophonous as she got in her licks:
Beast with two backs in the darkmans.)
                                        Then silence.
                                                    Trouble.
                                                            Himself
Charging into the light.
                        "Outa that!" (To the make-up man.)
"This sheet comes last till your high-building bastardboss pays up!"
(And McJoseph of the many-colored cadillac, gobbling his pasta in Florence,
Scheming to drive down the print cost, nibbling his caveat:
Master of pure thought: or at least the electronic equivalent.)
"Take that crap off the stone!"
                                One hour to go and now
Must wait for morning: for Mister T.'s high to blow over.
He goes out kneading his baby-bottom face: after the Cacajam
He slaps cologne on his jowls
                            —liniments of satisfied desire.

Thump.
            Wheezethump. Wheezethump.
                                        Thumpathump.
The pelagic banker.
                    The coupling she-crook.
                                            Patriot and whore.
Money at the bottom of the sea. . .
                                    Thump.
                                            Wheezethump.
                                                        Cacathump.

152

Nothing to do then but go out into the dark
Neon night of the soul, hillbilly the honky tonks and cheap
Ginmills of Santa Monica's Skid-Road-By-the-Sea.
Talk with the whores and the night cabdrivers; talk with Lo
(Bill Smoke by name) the poor Indian. Apache
And Cherrycow (Chiricaua) at that.

                                        Shipwrecked on this strange
Coast a war ago. Lost, here: like the others;
Doing his time.
                    And so we wait for morning and the light.

And then back to the printshop where time, hangover and avarice
Have had their way with Mister Twister.
                               The forms are locked up;
The presses roll.
                Thump.
                      Wheezethump.
                            Money: sea-changed.

And so till the last day and the parting of ways with J.J.
McJ.
        He'd had me prisoner while he was in Italy: myself
Saving his bacon from Coca and Twister. Then, returned
McJ, and no gratitude in that quarter (but time will wound
All heels).
                So on the last day stood at the open
Rear door of the shop watching the Pacific: ("Damn best
View of any printshop in the world," testifies Twister).
There, under a grey sky, grey, dandiacal:
The sea:
            its cuffs of lace
                      its infinitely extensible blue
Coffins, cold.
        Thump.
                  And out of that colorless heaven
Some poor mad whore falls a whirling praying
Ten stories.

Thump.

To give us our Daily News:

Written in blood all over my pants: too late for the press.

Thump.

O poor beat bitch.

Thump. Thump.

Wheeze-thump, money-thump, press-thump, fucka-thump, heart-thump, god-thump

Megathump, warthump, metathump.

Dig the graves.

Thump.

Thump thump thump thump thump thump.

Thump.

Thump thump thump thump thump.

Thump thump.

Thump thump thump thump.

Thump thump thump.

Thump thump thump.

Thump thump thump thump.

Thump thump.

Thump thump thump thump thump.

Thump.

THUMP THUMP THUMP THUMP THUMP THUMP—

THUMP THUMP THUMP THUMP THUMP THUMP

Thump.

Thump.

Thump.

The sound of the ax in the tree. . .

4.

Play or slavery. It's there surely in labor: the place

We went wrong. One place anyway. Put a blaze

Here.

Sixty percent for war and murder and the rest

Not worth the doing.

But it gets done.

154

                              Half the national product
Is guilt.
                    And all in the trap of the midnight slot machine
Of a politics with smokeless gunpower: for a criminal nation
Of the rich and the mighty within the nation, for a compromised country
Half dead at the bottom and rotten ripe on top.

But then (begun before Easter) in the axbright late winter cold
I cut wood.
                    Trees exploding around me. . .
                                        secret dynamite
Smuggled into their systems by the black Aquarian frosts.
I cut wood.
                    Dreaming of this.
                              This page. . .

And in spring broke new soil and Genya planted a garden:
That green enchantment, sprung from her loving hand I sang then: how
The vegetables please us with their modes and virtues.
                                        The demure heart
Of the lettuce inside its circular court, baroque ear
Of quiet under its rustling house of lace, pleases
Us.
          And the bold strength of the celery, its green Hispanic
¡Shout! its exclamatory confetti.
                                        And the analogue that is Onion:
Ptolemaic astronomy and tearful allegory, the Platonic circles
Of His inexhaustible soul!
                              O and the straightforwardness
In the labyrinth of Cabbage, the infallible rectitude of Homegrown
                                                  Mushroom
Under its cone of silence like a papal hat—
                              All these
Please us.
          And the syllabus of the corn,
                    that wampum,

155

                                                        its golden
Roads leading out of the wigwams of its silky and youthful smoke;
The nobility of the dill cool in its silences and cathedrals;
Tomatoes five-alarm fires in their musky barrios, peas
Asleep in their cartridge clips,
                              beets blood,
                                        colonies of the imperial
Cauliflower, and the buddha-like seeds of the pepper
Turning their prayerwheels in the green gloom of their caves.
All these we praise: they please us all ways: these smallest virtues.
All these earth-given:
                      and the heaven-hung fruit also. . .
                                                    As instance
Banana which continually makes angelic ears out of sour
Purses, or the winy abacus of the holy grape on its cross
Of alcohol, or the peach with its fur like a young girl's—
All these we praise: the winter in the flesh of the apple, and the sun
Domesticated under the orange's rind.
                                    We praise
By the skin of our teeth, Persimmon, and Pawpaw's constant
Affair with gravity, and the proletariat of the pomegranate
Inside its leathery city.
                        And let us praise all these
As they please us: skin, flesh, flower, and the flowering
Bones of their seeds: from which come orchards: bees: honey:
Flowers, love's language, love, heart's ease, poems, praise.

                         *   *   *   *   *   *

But that was later.
                  What was *then* was only the work and the waiting:
To find the first blaze:
                        to begin the lonesome labor
Of the resurrection man:
                        to elaborate my legend:
                                              to make
The Kachina. . .

156

                    Great clocks of the highs and lows tick out
The white weather
                    —and the windy angels of the compass points
Blow and blare under the night sky's blazing nocturnal
Powers and adornments. . .
                              Here I stop. I begin with identity
And seek the Wilderness Trace and the true road of the spirit.
I start alone with labor and a place.
                              Not much
                                   But at least
That.

IV

1.

Love and hunger: all is done in these signs or never
Done.
        Or done wrong.
                Blazes.
                       (Left or right.)

And when work goes wrong, love goes wrong.
                               And the other way also.
So:
    praise the green thing
                  in the hand
                          in the eye
                              in the
Earth!
        Perfect.
             And: the queenly women of our youth,
Middle age, old age, and the grand princesses
Of death
        if any such be
                  it clearly behooves us to praise
Most highly.
            Here, then:
                   Hear!
               I begin
                     with
Jenny.

                  *   *   *   *   *   *

    Moon in Virgo.
                Autumn over the land,
Its smoky light, its. . .
                hawkhover

                crowhover
                            its lonely distances
Taut with migrant birds and bodiless calls far — farther
Than noon will own or night
                    cloaked all in mystery of farewell.

Morning stirring in the haymow must: sour blankets,
Worn bindles and half-patched soogans of working bundle-stiffs
Stir:
      Morning in the swamp!
                  I kick myself awake
And dress while around me the men curse for the end of the world.

And it *is* ending (half-past-'29) but we don't know it
And wake without light.
                Twenty-odd of us — and very odd,
Some.
      One of the last of the migrant worker crews
On one of the last steam threshing rigs.
                  Antedeluvian
Monsters, all.
        Rouse to the new day in the fragrant
Barnloft soft hay-beds: wise heads, grey;
And gay cheechakos from Chicago town; and cranky Wobblies;
Scissorbills and homeguards and grassgreen wizards from the playing fields
Of the Big Ten: and decompressed bankclerks and bounty jumpers
Jew and Gentile; and the odd Communist now and then
To season the host.
           Stick your head through the haymow door —
Ah!
    A soft and backing wind: the Orient red
East. And a dull sky for the first faint light and no sun yet.

4:30. Time to be moving.

                    Into the barnfloor dark
I drop down the dusty Jacob's ladder, feeling by foot,
The fathomless fusty deep and the sleepy animal night
Where the horses fart, doze, stomp: teams of the early
Crewmen: strawmonkey, watermonkey (myself) and the grain haulers.
They snort and shift, asleep on their feet.
                              I go, carefully,
Down the dung-steamy ammonia-sharp eye-smarting aisle
Deadcenter: wary of kickers, light sleepers and vengeful wakers.

A sleep of animals!
              Almost I can enter:
                              where all is green,
Where the miles are shorter, the winters warmer, but the barbed fences
Higher, sharper, than for me:
                        where the devil is man or a wolf;
Where color drains from the flower in the smiling charm of the universal
Green; and the beautiful is the edible. . .
                              the dreams furry, far-ranging
Straightforward fore-and four-footed only; their boots, barn-battering,
Dream-burnished: O rutilant ruminant ruminative right beasts!
—Running the moon-long marches and meadows of the free range
Or racing their shadows in the hot noon or tree-shaded in the high
Afternoon heat: or at streams in the cool evening coming
To rake with their burning hooves their sunbright and cloud formed images
Magnificent. . .
                  and nuzzle their deeper selves in the lucent flow. . .
Muzzle velvet, mane of moonlight and lightning, tail
Of smoke and aching speed; and neck of hunger and thunder!
                                                  So
Themselves see themselves.
                        I too.
                        But, in the world
Of work and need that sacred image fails.
                              Here,
Fallen, they feed and fast and harrow the man-marred small acres
Dull; and dulled.

161

                    Alas, wild hearts, we have you now:
—Old plugs
            hayburners
                        crowbait
                                    bonesack
                                        —Hail!

Morning chores.
                    I fire up the lantern
                                    the hairy mysterious
Legend beasts leap full-formed out of the gold of the light!
All rational.

                    I go to the box-stall where wary Ringo
Sleeps with three eyes open and a mutiny under his heart
The size of his native Montana. Bronc. Half mustang half
Hellion. At fourteen years he's as old as I and ought to be
Wise—wiser. A rebel. I treat him with all respect,
Puffing the padded saddle onto his skinny back.
I lead him into the corral and mount. Docile. I wait—
Then nine buck-jumps to limber his joints and mine
And out the corkscrew lane at a gut-jolt gallop he goes!

No halt for the hillslope—he hurls himself runaway down
Taking great gulps of space in break-my-neck lunges: teaching me
Prayer: a prayer for tight cinches, for his crazy and eagle eye
To spot the leg-snapping gopher holes in his downhill flight.

Shouting, singing, praying—the hills shake to our sound.
O holy marvelous morning! Ecstatic plunge into fullest
Being! Blazing down to what end? None! To none!
But straight through the strait gate and into reality prime!

After the insane downslope dash he drops to a jog,
Lazy. Blows like a hairy whale. Nips at my leg—
Since he hasn't succeeded in killing me, we can be friends.

                    162

South toward the river in the brightening morning through the hill-held silence
—Or south toward the morning:
                              the heaven-high riverhills held at their tips
The green fur of the unfarmed sun in their tree-trap fingers
While we rode through the chilly lingering dusk of the coulee floor.
Such risings there!
                      The lorn jackrabbit kiting away
Husked from his buckbrush break; and out of their thin tents of grass
Partridge: smoking away on wings of wind and wet:
The dew collecting the vented light like vapor trails in their wake!
And the early snake
                  dry creek
                                carries his sand
South with us: cold trail-blazer: road in the high grass.

Southward all of us.
                      Then the river.
                                      The ancient song
Of cold stone and water.
                            Winds mouthing the trees
                                                    sigh. . .
And sacred silence
                  panic
                          structure of blood and change
Still mystery
            spills and holds.
                              Here, then.

The horses are hidden in thickets.
                                  Charge in like a brush-popper,
Stampede them out of the river trees and hooraw them home!
And in good time: the sky is building a fence of lightning
Over the hills; a door in the weather opens; light dies;
Wind and water burst out of the high house of the clouds—
The dust on my clothes still dry and I'm soaked to the skin!

Home, then: headlong
                    under the buckshot rain.

                              2.
Paradisaical morning! for the boy in a man's clothes!
                                        Heavenly
Rain-recess from the light-long labor in the harvest fields—
Pie-from-the-sky!

                    Shivering, I stable Ringo and run
For the lank unpainted house: its windows yellowly lit
In the second-come night of the rain-black morning's stormy show.
Enter headlong.
                    From the wood range the dark violence
Of oratorical coffee!
                    And eggs crackling heraldic
Voices in a hell of burnt bacon!
                              A Robinson Crusoe
Raft of toast in the warming-oven!
                              An alarm of onions
In the mansion of fried potatoes!
                         Apple pie!
                                   Cookies!
                                        Chow-chow!

And the cool cucumber stoned in his salt-and-vinegar broth!

At the head of the table: Parsons, the farmer we work for, owly
And sour with his twenty four apostles around him, seeing his provender
Devoured by these locusts in blue jeans: No work today
Rain says.
                    And Parsons sees us, hundred-headed eating
The roots of his house.
                         Dolorous dour.
                                   His gloom condenses
In the cellars of salt. Thickens. The stuff won't pour.

164

But O then:
Jenny!
Entering, the light swarms around her!
The rain
Ceases and the sun leaps out of the trap of wind and cloud!
And she enters: under the full sail of her breasts and body
Magical.
A poor Jane of a Sand Hill crane, maybe but
Jenny of the light blond hair
of the musical breasts
Of laughter warmer than sunlight and song like a moon-crazed bird!

What human Heisenberg principle made her possible who
Can say?
Came out of a Sand Hill farm that was blowing south
By acre and home forty each time the north wind raised.
Flower of poverty and ignorance—but a flower!
Each petal perfect.
And ripe. Or ripening outward as flowers and fruit ripen—
A woman with the sun in her belly and her own interior summer
Always at prime
and the yellowy winds of the summer solstice
Ripening her hair.
Woman like a Renaissance palace
grand plazas
Her ass, each part: or matchless mares of her buttocks perfectly
Matched: not either was faster
sculptured steeds in the vast
Apartments where the moon kept shop
little more than the size of your palm...

And this young queen was the hired girl, come in to serve us
In that holy morning.
Perhaps she was seventeen—she seemed
Old; to my almost-fourteen and woman-loverless years—
And wise.

Eve there.
                    Far.
                              Ancient.
                                        Knowing.
                                                  A mystery. . .
—Of what?
          Why what but first-off the mystery of holy Woman
And the mystery of her Mysterious East directly south of her belly
Button—all more mysterious from the spancelled and furious need
Of thirty celibate stiffs—and stiff we were when she brought us
The hearty heartening egg in its nest of chastened bacon.

And sweet she was also: her queenly coming-and-going—
Little canoe on the dark lake of the morning—brought us
The honey and lightning of a world outside our own brutal
Male thunder and mind-dulling labor.
                                        She came like a guide—
Some Indian princess: singing, exotic, prophetic. . .
                                                  occult
News—
          word of the high passes, the dark crossings
Over the bitter mountains in the months of snow. . .
                                                  —but the Word:
Blazes. . .
          in the masculine darkness funky. . .
                                        Sacagawea
Female kachina. . .
                    girl with a gift for making your pants
Too small in front.
                    Fine and superfine hung over our heads:
The bread and honey she brought us and the pure wine of her life!

*   *   *   *   *   *

And afterward the day of unwork opens: magical morning,
The rain-soaked earth steaming under a blow-torch sun.
Too wet for threshing!

166

                    The dice-doctors and the demon dealers
Drop the blanket, unseal the packs, make devil-deft passes—
Invite the multitude to a convocation of money.
                                                    Ada
From Decatur is there—and her tiny cousin: Little Joe
From Kokomo—and every defunctive and nadasymmetrical flush.

Meanwhile others are sousing their shirts in the nightblack iron
Enormous washpot that broods like a cancerous phoenix over
The moody backyard fire.
                        And the liars are lying and the lyres
Telling truth: auguries spelled out in the mantic entrails
Of travelling harmonicas musical threshing floors.
                                            O and the odd
Mildman mending his socks in the wash of enduring sun!

Now come the subtle apothecaries of the catch-as-catch-can concoctions:
Fabricators of Blast Head, Skinny and Forty Rod
(Will kill you at forty rods or stun you at half a mile)
Descanting and decanting the enchanted smoke of unjugged moonshine—
Milky dynamite of oily spoiled corn: coiled
Snake in the bog of a Mason jar: by coonlight lugged into
The twentieth century: that longest unfulfilled inside strait
Flush in history
                And the master-whittlers: carvers of fans,
Creators of piny Granadas from the lace of lazy wood!
And wooing in the watertrough-shade-Workers'-University: the spadehanded
Fellow-worker-comrade-professor expressing Marx!
                                            And Mumbley
Peg! Like a gypsy dream of flashing wild knives!
And airborne the rhyming chime of clashing horseshoes mock silver
Filling the stunned light that yet runs from there to Arcturus:
And ourselves, strange travellers, still live on that starry beam. . .

And so the morning. . .

                    wearing a bright bandana like a Mexican
Bandit

          wears away.
                    And along about quarter-time comes
My call: to go out into the late corn and gather
The gold and pearl of the roasting ears for the noon meal.
—And there she was—Jenny!—filling the field with light
Brighter than sun!
                    And so we labored together—that action
Nearest to love: when work is play.
                              And around us the spires
Lifting
        the living green
                          a music of hoarse rattles,
The whispering pipes and the feathery cymbals of the fiery field
Swaying ripening song: silky answer to a cadence
Of the flattering wind.
                        And there we opened the holy wigwams and hogans—
Pulled back a tent-flap of husk to peer at the seated and sacred
Congregation
              grandfather maize. . .
                              ear in the milk!
We snap them loose from the stalk and pop them into the sack.

Sack? There was none but the front of Jenny's dress
Lifted.
          Over a mystery: where the bronze and pearl frontiers
Divided sun from moon on her downy meridian thighs. . .
And singing so in holy labor, soon we came
To the end of the shallow field, where the old willow kept,
Over the coulee heights, his whispering watch. . .
                                        Rested there. . .
Then—out of pure gift for my thirteen-plus-nothing-years-need
Opened her dress!
                  stepped forth!

                              moon coming out of a cloud!
—And lay beside me
                    warm as a star coming into my arms!
And we made love
              in the damp grass
                            under the willow. . .
I entered her
              opening the silky gate and passing through
The marvellous terrible thighs to the ancient and aweful world
Mysterious
            full of the rituals and terrors of men. . .

                                    and found there
This girl. . .
              innocence. . .
                          laughter. . .
                                found my self. . .
Seemed to.
              We rode each other to the opposite ends of the earth:
And arrived together in the sacred terminal of holy commerce—
Place where one can arrive only by two's and two
Is one or nothing. . .
                  blazing there. . .
                              in the damp grass. . .

And lying beside my darling girl, my hand on the bush of her belly
The whole enormous day collected within my palm. . .
Around us the birds were singing their psalms, and the bent grass
Shyly unkinked the joints we had lovingly flattened.
                                      The air
Grew warm and round around us: but the wheeling sun rolled fast.

At last she left; like a goddess: bearing against her belly
The fruit of the chanting enchanted field and my own invisible sign.
Ah, there was a girl come along early to wake me

Out of the wintry sleep of boyhood: to take her hand
—And mine!—into countries where all may journey but only
Without maps
                without compass
                                riding blindfold. . .
—And she took me into the country of strangers and enemies, the violent
World of men! And it was. . .
                                innocence
                                        love
                                                the world
Of children again
                but bigger only
                                and I was older
Already than any.

                She left me there, god's years later—
A half hour, maybe—her lap heavy with daylight.
And I lay in our musky couch counting the fields of the sky. . .
Love enhungered love; but unhungered hunger for the hungering
Hungry boy.
                For the time being—or always?—I lived on
Slow dreams under the willow where the milkweed pod
Opens a feathery eye toward the bird-breathing sun. . .

                    *   *   *   *   *   *

At quarter time in the afternoon, roused; returned
To the barnyard.
                My head full of honey and the flag of my loins aloft.
Lifted myself on the haymow ladder and poked my head
Into the upper dark. . .
                saw there. . .
                                "Not for kids—
We're separatin' the men from the boys here!" Rod speaking
The boss spike-pitcher. "Git down outa this, boy! Git down!"
He pushes me down the ladder and drops the trap door shut.

                            170

But I had seen
                    there in the musty dark
                                        Jenny—
Or another Jenny. . .
                    (Moon coming out of a cloud!)
                                                  Her cloudy
Transfigured flesh in the gloom!
                                    (On a lance of light from a knothole
The dust was dancing, aloft, on the spunky smell of their sex,
Where they swelled around her like animals drawn to the Christmas-manger—
French-postcard.)
                    And her face—poor face!
                                              (That was open, loving, wild
Under the willow in the greeny light) like a breathing trap
Shut now.
            Locked as in terrible combat.
                                          She lay
Bucking under some loud clown with his pants still on.
Suffering
            acting
                    burning
                                entranced
                                            cold
                                                  dedicated. . .

Ladies' choice!
                A gang-bang,
                                But there was no arm-twisting—
She wanted it so.
                    I stood deadstill in the barndoor dirt
(Hearing the overhead thump and thinking of sweating quarters
Of dying meat upstairs
                          those souls
                                        consumed and consuming)
Stunned in the rain-cleared light as if I'd been kicked by a horse,
Hurting.

What hath god rot?

What hath Rod

Got?

Friend, when all collapses around you the bosses
Find work.

So, with Bill Dee and Ed, the midnight twins,
Into the bonerattling blank field to clean the boiler
Of the ancient Nichols and Shepherd steamer stonily sitting
(And the hole in the whistle alone weighed seventeen pounds on a Sunday!)
On its tenfoot wheels like an indolent idol.

Before Freud came
To North Dakota we did it: ramming the brushended rods
Down the fifteen foot slots of the grimy honeycomb flues.

Symbolical day!

And philosophy shot on the wing!

"Take now,"
(Ed says) (groaning a little) "them Sand Hill girls.
Stay away from there, little buddy. Them women will give you a dose
Before you can spell gangkorea, man! They'll clap you up
Ere you can bring your pants to half mast. I *mean* it—
And if I don't know who does? Measure is all," says Ed.

"Measure yourself to that fire-box," Bill Dee tells me. "Get in there!"
I slither in like a rattler, the fire-door shaking its tail,
And the chimes fall in the flat field like a handful of silver.
"You think you got *troubles*," Bill snorts. He pops out his glass eye.
"Stick this here up your ass and see what the world looks like!
And say me no aye, yes or nay but sing it out plain!"

Inside the iron womb of the firebox' small world I look:
The wall frescoed with scale:

flamepainted murals

I cannot

Read.

I crouch there.

This roaring castle of fire

                              —cool now—

Around which revolves the world of the rig on the days of our labor.
"How's old iron cunt?" Bill calls.

                              And gentler, to my ears only,

Through the metal lip of the fire door: "It's many a good man
Got up on the wrong side of an Indian pony. . ."

                                             trying

To help me understand.

                         I cannot.

                              I take up the poker,

Knock the clinkers loose from the grates and slam open the damper.

After they leave I fire up the old lady—the new water,
Cold in her belly, must warm for the next day morning run.
I peel the rain-wetted skin from the strawmonkey's rack and feed
The quilted clot of the tweedy flaxstraw into her stony womb;
Scratch a match on my pants and the end of the fire-blacked fork
Blazes; (the oily flax, crackling, blows out the daylight)
I put the torch through the iron lips and a great roar
Breaks loose from the lion of fire inside the door slot!

                                             Open the damper.

Let him rave.

            Then steady

                  fork after fork

                              each one

Left in the slot till it lights and the fire burns inside and out.
As she warms I test the water injector: blast out shrieking clouds
Of blistering steam.

                  She draws.

                              Give the old lady a drink,

Open the blowers and cram her belly with incendiary flax,
Button her up and *done*!

                  I turn away from the dark-bringing
Fire half-blind (and the fire still blazing under my eyelids)!

Amazed that the day still stays and the skyborne westtilted field
Lifting late sunlight. . .
                         and the lag-along birds homebound to treeclaims
Lofting to kin and mankind the shy spiel of lark song
Dove song
          crow call
                    far-faring
Sparrow. . .
          the loose ends of the evening.
                                        I stood there
Elaborate loneliness
                    like an unfinished Navajo blanket
                                                   empty
As the threshed field
                    lost as some fabulous gold mine
                                                  hollow
As an abandoned tunnel. . .
                         high and far the sky
Stood over me and my small woe.
                              Distant voices,
Indifferent, drifted in on the cold of the autumn evening.
I turn to go: reluctant: at leaving the orderly orders
Of labor and this manageable iron maiden, her clanking pulse, her
Cud of fire and cloud.
                    I crank up the balky truck,
I turn, and, flat wheeled and rattling, drive down the breathing field.

*   *   *   *   *   *

That night they broke Outlaw — were breaking him when I came back,
A buckskin bronco — hammer-headed, wall-eyed, long-gaited and loco —
Mean as a runaway buzzsaw: kicker, striker and biter
Beautiful! Totally useless. Kept around maybe as Parson's
Secret sin. Or hope. And for years Outlaw had broken
Presumptive cowpokes, persuading them out of the west.
                                                  And now —
Three ropes to hold him and still rearing!

But they ear him down,
Snub him against the corral-post and slap the blindfall on. . .
Stiff-legged he stands there quivering, as if there were fire under
The creamy skin.
   Now saddle. . .
      now cinch. . .
         tight. . .
            tighter
Too tight. . .
    Now hackamore on and rider up and blindfold
Off!

  The honyock pulls leather at the first stone-legged buckjump;
Outlaw swaps ends like a blacksnake: while the rider is openly wondering
Whether to shit or go blind.
      Then a lazy, sunfishing, slow
Roll like a dolphin empties the saddle.
        And so he sends them—
And this in the sloughfooty bog the rain has made the corral!
Drunk sober or sane, the long the short and the tall—
He shucks them out of the saddle like popping peas from a pod!

But not forever.
    In the leg-locking mire of the barn corral
They rode him.
    Rode him at last—Rod did—had to be him!—
Poor-devil Outlaw stoned with fatigue trying his best
To rear over backward and Rod smashing his ears down
With the loaded quirt.
    Myself: silent:
      screaming:
       Outlaw!

Outlaw! Outlaw! Tear your foot free from the earth!

    *   *   *   *   *   *

And light years later in the haymow loft I lay.
                                        Long-
Remembering Jenny. . .
                        My ding-dong darling and haymow madonna. . .
Sexual vessel
            lay for us
Vessel of singular ardor
                    screw for us
Horizontal rose   carburetor most holy   princess of poontang
Two stroke virgin   independent suspension   unholstered cunt
            help us in the hour of our need
Long-cock echo-chamber   uterine superhighway most travelled
            accept our offerings
Candid receptacle
                receive our prayers
Hairy gate
            open for us
Bridge of thighs
                carry us over
Encyclopedic pudenda   hairy prairie,   automated vagina
                                    Be with us in the day of our hunger

ENOUGH!
            Even then I could see it was not that way.
                                        She was no
Gongshagging lamewit.
                    But then what was she?
                                        Easy: merely
Lost.
        And what did she want?
                        To enter.
                                To burn
Alive. . .
            To live on other frequencies, at more intolerable depths. . .
To rip up the tent of solitude, to step out of the skin,
To find among the damned the lost commune and to found there,
Among the lost, the round song and the psalm of the living world.

176

And I too had entered those latitudes of desperation and given
Through her (or earlier): my heart to the lost ones of the world
Forever.
            Sad, that bridge of bodies, trying to build
On mere number the Great Aleph of solidarity. . .
And I see them still. . .
                    bang-tail babes in death-dark drag
In the Village or in Little East Nowhere North Dakota
                         or Lost
Angels in Super Scab's smog-lined mafioso scout-camp Venice L.A. . . .
It's lack-love set this blaze. . .
              in this sad country where number
Counts
       where love has no hands. . .
                no fingers. . .
                    (but I remember,
When I take my death in my hands to write and endite you this,
Or climbing the terrible stairs of the typewriter to hang
By the skin of my heart to the cold col, to cross over
To the true blaze).

          I didn't know, then, it's the Innocents
Who must live most lost, most reckless. . .
                the life of a dangerous time.

      *   *   *   *   *   *

Midnight. . .
        the great nets of the stars. . .
                sifting the darkness.
Night birds.
      A whine of wind.
          That's all there really is. . .
Except for the mind's excitement, the heart's hill-hurdling desire,
But at that age it seemed not enough. The world seemed empty. . .

Wind out of the north quadrant.
                                        Clear.
                                                The barometer
Lifting a wing of salt and sun. . .
                                        work in the morning.

                                3.
The great fires in the heavens whirl and wheel.
                                                The wind
Shifts.
            The continental circuses of calm and storm blow
Through our houses.
                        The hurrying years collect in the counting rock. . .

I met Marian on the road to a war and we held hands
Over the dead.
                    And after. . .
                                    when I returned from the long
Enchantment.
                Or someone returned. . .
                                            wearing my used body.
— Girl with the moon in her pocket!
                                    Quail-keeping girl
                                                        girl
With the red-eared hound. . .
                            That innocent
                                        perfect. . .
                                                    — returned and left her,
Torn away in the vast cyclone of the Post War, the psychotic
Continental drift
                    the heart torn out of my side.
                                            I had met
My own Dark Lady.

                    And of that time, as of records

Kept, etc.
       as of marked stones left on the trail
                    as of blazes
                          or gardens
Planted and tended
       —it's all in Sauvequipeutville, Salsipuede
Avenue Marsh Street Elysian Valley. . .
                twenty feet under
The progressive concrete where the freeway came through.
                      And the world rides
Over a poor house, bulldozed down and buried.

What I met looked like a mask (dead-set for early death,
With the mask of insanity under it) made from the money-of-the-month.
—Mask of a rich whore, a bourgeoise, chippying around
With the dangerous world of the poor.
              Pulled off that mask and found there—
(The damned call out to the damned: "Save me!"
                Cry I can never deny). . .
—In the woman of our fatality, we find under the mask
Ourselves
      our own lost innocence
           crying to be redeemed.

In that mirror of flesh we confront our own past
(Which is always wrong)
         our weakness
            (therefore: terror, despair)
Our own corruptibility
        our human potential for being
Lost.
   And *that* woman is all the mortal hungers
Of our own lost years;
       our defeats;
         our secret country;

Childhood
　　　　　future
　　　　　　　　hope
　　　　　　　　　　fear
　　　　　　　　　　　　class
　　　　　　　　　　　　　　revolution
Our fate.

　　　　　　　In those days we built our cooking fire
On the wind
　　　　　　　walked only over the abyss
　　　　　　　　　　　　slept, always
In a vast bed swinging among the polar stars.
In those days we invented the atlas of handy catastrophe;
Discovered the buried languages hidden under the twelfth rib—
The illuminated jokes of the Cardinal of Lower Mombasa;
　　　　　　　　　　　　　　projected
(Only on astral planes it is true) the psychic structures
Of the mechanical grand pianos that were grinding Mozart to death.
What did we care that Mexican calendars were full of antique
Firecrackers?
　　　　　　　The A-bomb shelters full of lepers, the banks
Leprous with exploding money?
　　　　　　　　　　　The bed swung round with the world
But we lay always true north like needles of blood and bone.

And each to other like a wall, world, electric fence—
Bluebook　secret-society　conspiracy　cartel　enchanted castle. . .
Assaulting each other to extremes of flesh, like holy burglars
Breaking into a Saracen keep in search of the Holy Grail.
We had to smash all masks and tear down every wall.

These hungers fed only on themselves.
　　　　　　　　　　　Each road was chosen
Only for its dangers: the desperate authentication of terror
That kept the world at bay.

For when love becomes the Absolute
It cannot admit that Other, and it longs always for death:
That final seal on its value and condition the lovers aspire to
Because changeless.
                    They dream to burn there.
                                        Perfect,
                                                And perfectly
Unmoved and unmoving.
                    Radiant.
                                The point at the heart of the diamond. . .

But fate never asked us to die for the revolution or love.
And the world got in the way at last, the world of the blacklist,
Of money and need in a bourgeois town.
                                        In time it finished us off.

                        *   *   *   *   *   *

"I've seen it many's the time," (Martin speaking, my brother)
"That riverboat gambler aristocrat with the flowery vest
Headin' out west with his TB and a double-eagle on his watch chain,
To burn like a damned soul in Tombstone or Dodge City,
Reckless, gallant, lost.
                        But they all sober up in the end.
They wind up in Azusa: putting the lawn under concrete
And painting it green.
                        My god, man, don't you *ever* watch teevee?
That's just life on the Great Pubic Plains, old buddy!"
And Peets is adding: "If'n you cain't eat it or screw it, fuck it!"

Maybe may be.
                    The world is too much but not enough with us. Soon-later
Most give up or go under—
                                terrible erosion in the gaunt
Seasons.
            In the killer winds.

And we are flesh, not rock.
But must be.
The gentle rock:
not to wear out;
to stand
Against Frivol, Trivil, and Superfice, the three national giants—
And to stand there in the tearing wind when all seems lost:
Our life shot down at a distance: death of a hungry wolf. . .

*   *   *   *   *   *

And so I must praise and pray for all loved lost women,
The queens of the green years.
Time filled them with babies,
Wore down their loving hands
emptied their mouths of kisses,
And led them into the dust at the foot of the grandfather stair. . .

There, leave them in peace
who were so lovely once.

4.
Little as it is, what have we, comrades, but love and the class struggle?
The rock and the wind and the drifting delegate blazes of fellow
Travellers.
stars
our far and fiery companions. . .
and nothing
To wear but this angry body: of which only one is issued
And always too big or too small
—always too *hungry*—
and the angry
Hungering soul. . .
—and *that*. . .

never the right size either. . .

You only live twice: once in the mind and once
In the world.
                    But, in the world, only the unexpected
Happens, ever.
                    And so I was given a second chance
And the girl came:
                    Genia:
                            of innocence
                                        beauty
                                                valor. . .

She found me there — this child did — on a road deadset
For death
            and turned me
                            compassionate compass of flesh
                                                    O fiery
Heart
        O treasure of warmth in the bourse of ice
                                        O
Companion and stranger
                    miner's-light
                                lighthouse of the temporal sea. .
This same sea I saw say early and slowly:
(Men low lie here: crazed: and crazy they laze and die —
Lo! Death) lost-night's-life away only, uttering a cold corpse, say:
    — Love
            It's bells   barks   bridges.
                                    Its midnight sun. . .

All this in a girl with a handful of debts, a black cat, an upright
Piano full of theories, heresy, heartache, dynamite-violets?
And each white key a doorway to the world's anguish and each
Black key a gate, a hurled stone, a wild horse,
And each horse named and each name known and the knowledge filed
Under each white key for to ride the straight of those lonesome roads
Alone in the dark or the shine of the long or the wrong ways
In the light of the runaround moon?

It was so.
                              And each
Day of her life like a loaded sail — and no wind in sight! —
And each sail two ships; and each ship
A white ship or a black ship; and each
White ship a hope; and each black ship
A promise; and each sail loaded
                              with dynamite. . .
                                             cats. . .
And ravening grand pianos
                    will grab you
                                     simply because
You walk around at blood-heat.
                              Heatseekers.
                                       Was it?
                                             It was,
So.
     And not so.
                    She was a second life that I might have
Wasted.
          Too close to say. . .
                         The life I put on over
My death.
          The second heart that was given me in place of that other
I wore too long on my poor flag.
                              Yes.
                              It was so.

And so I entered again the growth of innocence.
                                     And, writing —
Now! — I am furry with animal light.
                                   I enter the ecstatic
Round dance of the fox and the field mouse on the scarred, warring
Hills,
          the rites of passage toward the sacred city of birdsong,
The tunnels of morning hunger and the ancient rivers of night. . .

And now here she is sleeping. . .

                  the arch of her foot darkened. . .

By the passing of time, by the oil of the classic sea. . .

                      and outside

This window

        in the halt of the afternoon

                in the Skyrian light

A sewing machine of birds is mending a side of the weather

Which the locusts unravel hourly in the clattering heat.

                      And outside

This window

        midnight

              the white and faultless moon riding

The snowy hills and fields of Dakota.

            And she lies sleeping!

Under all this burden!

        Kachina. . .

            blazes. . .

                and blessings!

V

1.

Man is the fate of his place and place the fate of the man
And of time. . .
                    Had arrived there
                              — North Dakota, the farmhouse
                                                      the old

Dominion of work and want (but all in a new style now)
My turnaround point and old time stomping ground
To find the place we went wrong and blaze the trail through the dark,
To make the kachina. . .
                    night   journey   inbound   dream
Voyage. . .

              *   *   *   *   *   *

              The road outside the window was "our" road
Once. It is now anybody's road.
                              It is the road
On which everyone went away.
                              Take it.
                                        To the coulee bottom —
Head south on the ice toward the Indian graves and the river.

Sunday.
        Calm as a saint
                    and the church-bells falling like wounded
Parachutes into the parochial dark of St. Mary's-at-Sheldon into
The noonday acetylene of snow and sun as I tramp south.

The coulee holds, at the far end, a black bone
In its mouth: the river trees: sheathed in a plating of sleet,
And I hear, in the cold hush, their icy rosaries clicking
A mile of frozen Aves.

                    Little changed, or changing —
River: still wild: earth hold here
(As always I hope) the glamour of animal night, the holy
Terror of empty places, secret, and the ancient pre-human
Light.
                    Luminous, the river snow unscrolls a white
Tall, tell-tale: faint script of bird and hieroglyph of beast:
Where one has come to a dead end in the air as the owl,
Falling, trolled him away; or hawk struck; or the stalking
Mink closed and clung in his hunger.
                                        In the stark up-river
Sun I see the black of the beaver town where my youngest
Brother (dead now) trapped the old bulls in a happier winter.

The beaver have moved since those times; have come downstream
Toward easier forage.
                    A short walk on cold water
Takes me here: by a dam-site. And here I sight in the up-stream
Black and blaze the place I swam one long gone midnight
After setting the threshing rig in the neighbor field.
                                                Glareice
Above the dam where the last thaw run-off froze.
                                                Listen:
Under the skin of dark, do I hear the singing of water?
The trees tick and talk in the almost windless calm
And the stream is spinning a skein of an old and lonesome song
In the cold heart of the winter
                              constant still.
                                        One crow
Slowly goes over me
                    — a hoarse coarse curse
                                        — a shrill
Jeer: last of the past year or first of the new,
He stones me in appalling tongues and tones, in his tried
And two black lingoes.
                    A dirty word in the shine,

A flying tombstone and fleering smudge on the winter-white page
Of the sky, my heart lightens and leaps high: to hear
Him.
       And the silence.
                    That sings now: out of the hills
And cold trees.
         Song I remember.

                       I turn to the slope
That lifts to the bench, taking a path that the rabbits broke
In their moon-crazed rambles.
                I grope for handholds in the buckbrush clumps,
I thumb the horny gooseberry brittle: stiff in his winter
Dress
     — grab on and climb.
               A rime of icy crystal
Glitters around my going like sun-maddened precious stones!

A step; a half-step, and a step more. I finally make it
Over the shallow lip and stand on the low plateau:
Here's Tommy Comelately to pore over the bones
Another time.
          And what's here — on the little bluff
Over the little river?
            A way station, merely;
A half-way house for the Indian dead — analphabetic
Boneyard. . .
          It was here the Sioux had a camp on the long trail
Cutting the loops of the rivers from beyond the Missouri and Mandan
East: toward Big Stone Lake and beyond to the Pipestone Quarry,
The place of peace.
         A backwoods road of a trail, no tribal
Superhighway; for small bands only. Coming and going
They pitched camp here a blink of an eye ago.

It's all gone now—nothing to show for it.
                                        Skulls
Under the permanent snow of time no wind will lift
Nor shift. . .
                    —these drifting bones have entered the rock forever. . .

And all done in the wink of an eye! Why my grandmother saw them—
And saw the last one perhaps: ascending the little river
On the spring high water in a battered canoe.
                                        Stole one of her chickens
(Herself in the ark of the soddy with the rifle cocked but not arguing)
Took the stolen bird and disappeared into history.

And my father, a boy at Fort Ransom, saw them each spring and fall—
Teepees strung on the fallow field where he herded cattle.
Made friends and swapped ponies with a boy his own age—
And in the last Indian scare spent a week in the old fort:
All the soddies abandoned, then.
                        Wounded Knee—
The last fight—must have been at that time.
                                        And now
All: finished.
            South Dakota has stolen the holy
Bones of Sitting Bull to make a tourist attraction!

From Indians we learned a toughness and a strength; and we gained
A freedom: by taking theirs: but a real freedom: born
From the wild and open land our grandfathers heroically stole.
But we took a wound at Indian hands: a part of our soul scabbed over:
We learned the pious and patriotic art of extermination
And no uneasy conscience where the man's skin was the wrong
Color; or his vowels shaped wrong; or his haircut; or his country possessed of
Oil; or holding the wrong place on the map—whatever
The master race wants it will find good reasons for having.

                *   *   *   *   *   *

190

The wind lifts and drones on the hill where a file of whispering
Snow wears at the bench-slope, rattling the sleet-stiff buckbrush,
And a train of cloud piles down from the high north,
Hiding the sun.
                    The day collapses toward evening.
                                        Cold,
I turn from the bone-white field and drive my feet toward home.

In the thickening early gloom the first of the night hunting
Begins.
            On a quickening wing, a Great Snowy Owl,
Pure as a mile of Christmas, sifts and seethes down the sky,
And the shy and hiding rabbit hears and turns his white softness
To stone.
            Tranced, fear serves and saves him.
                                        The owl steers over,
Swings out on a spur of wind, swerves in his search and is gone.

Snow on the wind.
                    First farmlight.
                                        In downriver darkness.
A fox barks.
                Once.
                        Again.
                                Silence and snow. . .
—And the fisherman still alive in the future in Skyros!
                                            (But dead
Now and forever.)
                    In the boneyard. . .
                                    Simulacra. . .
                                        The Indian is the first
Wound.

                                2.
            Evening—another evening—and the lights flare
From the farmstead yardlamps far over the blank open

191

Spread of the prairie night.
                              Renaissance of illumination
Courtesy REA.
                    And each lamp beacons and beckons
Across the neighbor and empty fields: *Come ye over.*
But no one comes.
                              And the traveller on the worn and improved roads
Goes by in improved darkness not even a barking dog
Lights. . .
                    The houses blacked out as if for war, lit only
With random magnesium flashes like exploding bombs (TV
Courtesy REA)
                    Cold hellfire
                              screams
Tormented, demented, load the air with anguish
                                        invisible
Over the sealed houses, dark, a troop of phantoms,
Demonic, rides: the great Indians come in the night like
Santa Claus
          down the electronic chimneys whooping and dead. . .

Still, in the still night from a high hill (if there were one)
In the dark of the moon, with the far and fiery heavensteads blazing —
Huge galaxy-ranches and farm-constellations and solitary starcrofts shining —
On such a night, if one had a hill, he might see, in these lower
And faster fields, the constellations of farmlight: less vast
But moving still, in their hour and season, like the Plough and the Bear
Burning. . .
          impermanent. . .
                              companions. . .
                                        Having their dignity there.

But from that imagined hill I see also the absence of light —
The abandoned farmhouses, like burnt-out suns, and around them
The planetary out-buildings dead for the lack of warmth, for the obscured
Light that the house once held.

And where has it gone?

And where

Have *they* gone? Those ghosts who warmed these buildings once?

Over the hills and far away. ("Our road"
Is anybody's road now: road that we all went away on.)
Away to the new wars, and the new ways, and the old
Whores of a system that found us expendable; to Work and to Want
In other pressures

playpens

—in wilder parts of the sky. . .

Dark, dark the houses lie there.

The wind of the winter,
Like an animal, tears at the broken roofs,

and the rain of spring
Opens the doors sly as a thief;

and the fires of summer,
Flare on the broken panes, blister, consume;

and autumn
Arranges in those sad parlors, chiefly, the melancholy
Of absent chairs.

There, hysteria has entered the wallpaper:
It flaps in the gloom like a trapped bird.

In empty kitchens
The rat-turds, hard as beebees, rust.

Filth on the stairs
(O grandfather dust!) thick and mousetracked, leads to rooms
Without character: boxes of boxed darkness: birdshit—
(But only the swallow nests here—the daubs of mud over doorways
Are the most live things in the house.)

In the downcellar dark
Are nests of Mason jars: crocks; jugs—an entire
Breakable culture abandoned archeological disjecta
Membra lost processes. . .

                              And the attic night trembles
For its terrible treasures
                                its secret histories like deadmen's bones
Unburied in the gapthroated oldfashioned trunks' dark fathoms.

Here, furbearing bibles, inlaid with fake gemstones,
Like sand covered drift-fences of tallies of a winter count,
Record, before Genesis, the early departures and the first begots—
Writ by hand. . .
                        and the letters, packaged in rotting twine,
Talk all dark in a language of leaving and loss
                                            forgotten
Tongues
            foreign
                    sounding
                            —words of love and hunger. . .

Finally the aging and ageless photographs, unfixed in time
Or light, mourn: for the abandoned ghosts who no longer
Haunt these frames.
                        And where have they gone?
                                            Through bankruptcy;
To be spiritual props to the interest rate in the Farmers' First
National Bank of West Nowhere Dakota;
                                    to die in the dying
She-towns of the farmlands and the thousand widow-sodalities
Of those depths (the husbands long gone under from working
To assure their wives this final loneliness).
                                        Last, they've gone
Back to the land:
                    in ten thousand little lost graveyards, forgotten:
Before the fashionable collectivity of contemporary death. . .

But you will not find them there, nor even the ruined stone
Maybe, that spelled their fate.

                    (Look for MacCormick reapers,
Look for the brass-tongued Nichols & Shepherd steamer these dead
Machines are more alive.)
                    And now where the fence lines join,
In deserted coigns and corners abandoned they enter the night rock. . .
In the lilac-choked encampments of the older dead, in a grave plot
(Where in summer the wheat like a bright sea breaks and in winter the fallow
Encroaches) under the last of the true prairie, the last
Of the wild grass.
                Forgotten.
                    Lost as the last Indian:
Who were good men in their time: a century or a cemetery ago.

                *   *   *   *   *   *

Leave 'em lay where Jesus flang 'em.
                            Turn away:
From these exhausted houses toward those newer lights,
Brighter but farther spaced than the old, with a greater emptiness
Between, around.
            In the deep
                    winter
                            rentier
                                    wheatrancher—
Who fed on those old bones   gone:
                        to Acapulco:
With their newest Janes in their bluest jeans to New Orleans
In their flying machines
                    (and they have 'em)
                                to Coeur d'Alene for the snow.
Or gone into the neighbor frau by way of a wife-swapping key-club—
And *herself* gone to shop in nearby Dementia via *Town and Country*
To return, after years of hunting in the haunts of artistical queens.
Covered with gay wall-papers wild and a flair for hysteria:
And all to adorn an unused den for a country bourgeois!
For the dead, *all else* is alive.

                    Or how explain
The bourgeois belief in a boss culture?

                                  But most I see
(Between the magnesium flashes cold, before the dawn's early
Light) the sad sons of the prairie: sitting in darkness.
There, in a glass, brightly, they sleep on two sides at once:
The past, the future: at last united.
                                  (Courtesy R E
A.)   A moment.
                A kind of sleep.
                              Clear to the end.
Where?
          Here.
                This is one end of the night
                                          now.

But no present: only the past and the future: both false.
As the poet saith (Bob Bly) drawn down
The barrels of inexhaustible revolvers to sleep like freaks
In the .45 caliber interchangeable wombs alcohol
Insulated
            at home
                    TV

                  Dakota
                        is everywhere
                                and *grow* there
Like the jolly white giant
                      in intolerable pressures
                                        at home
                                            in the expanding
Expendible universe grown at ease
                              with the Indians' end

And their own
                some future
                               pi in the sky
                                        it's here already.
And the missiles
                  Minot
                        Grand Forks
                                   sleeping their murderers' sleep. . .

                        3.

And the people?
                "First they broke land that should not ha' been broke
                                            and they *died*

Broke. Most of 'em. And after the tractor ate the horse—
It ate *them*. Most of 'em. And now, a few lean years,
And the banks will have it again. Most of it. Why, hellfar,
Once a family could live on a quarter and now a hull section won't do!
Half of the people gone left the country; the towns dyin';
And this crop uh hayseeds gutless—wouldn't say shit and themselves
Kickin' it out their beds. It's hard lines, buddy!"

Bill Dee speaking his piece: hard times
In the country.
                  Bill Dee: last of the old bronc-stompers
From the gone days of Montana mustangs we used on the farms
For light work and for riding and the pure hell of having
Outlaws around. . .
                      The same Bill Dee of the famous removable
Eye: which he'd slip in your shot-glass sometimes—O blinding and sobering
Sight!
              —"Just take a swally uh *that* and say what yer innards
Perdick fer the follyin' winter! Take a *glass* eye view of the world 'n
Change your luck!"
                    Not only a glass eye: a gab
Nine miles longer than a telephone wire.

A sense of style:
Could roll cigarettes on a bucking horse in a high wind —
But only one-handed of course. . .
                              Was the greatest success I know
Out of the old days alive
                    alone
                    but alive —
Had decided he wanted to be a broncsnapper and cowboy and *made* it —
On the last ranch on the hither side of the moon.
                                        And lived there
Still: on the Bonesack.
                    (Ranch in the Sand Hills.)
                                        And a small cabin
Built there: of elm and cottonwood made: squatter —
"Ain't a hell of a lot, but it's more 'n some got: *'n hol' that, Tiger!*"
He rattles on as we rattle along in his ancient car,
And that's where we're heading: down to the Hills in the late-winter day.

Under the thin snow the Hills show no sign
Of natural order.
                    Sand from a post-glacial delta, the winds
Pushed them into no pattern, and now the grass half-holds
These random structures: holds for our lives' long moment only,
Perhaps.
                    Under the noon-high sun the blow-outs' sandwhite
Eyes glare back at the cold light.
                              The sun clots
In the bunched buckbrush, is caught in a patch of briar and bramble —
And a deer jumps out of the light, flies over a fence, sails
Across the top of a hill like a puff of cloud!
                                        "*That* one,
I'm savin' a while yet," Bill says: as if it were something he owned.

Scrub oak on the hills; chokecherry; staghorn sumac
By the river's edge. . .

                    and there the ancient and moving order
Of the living water: now ranged in its wintry keep.
                                        Where the bluff drops
Steeply down toward the ice are the sedgy halls and freeholds
Of mink and muskrat on the swampy ground and then the river.

"Old Sheyenne got better fishin' each year," Bill says.
"Them honyocks around here just too *lazy* to fish. They druther
Buy them damn *froze* fish in them plastic bags.
Why, hellfar, you remember that place where that spring comes in —
Nigh my cabin? Used to take fish out of there with *scoop* shovels —
Gunnysacksful! 'n people with pitchforks spearin' the big uns!
They don't fish there no more — nobody but me. Why, boy,
We get you some whoppin' Northerns 'n the best-eatin' goddam Walleyes —
Takes an illegal net to get illegal fish, 'n I *got* one!"
Illegal fish flesh and fowl — about all that he lives on.

And into the Hills lost places: now, following
The river, and again buckjumping over the iron, faceless
Ranchroads: opening the gates in the fences, kittycornering and quartering
The waste. . .
              Dead houses here in the bottom lands:
                                        an eyeless
Schoolhouse, abandoned, crumbles;
                              undenominational forever,
A church is stumbling into an empty future, lofting
A headless and rotting Christ on the cracked spool of a cross:
Unspinning god at a loss in the psalm of the man-eating wind.

"Ever'body here got blown out in the last of the dusters.
Should never been farmed no-way. The country's sure empty. But me —
I like it this way.
                   And the animals comin' back! Why, hellfar,
They ain't only pheasant and grouse — man, there's wild *turkey*.
There's deer, there's foxes, there's — last night I swear I heard a coyoot —
Heard it or dreamed it. . . They're comin' back sure — the old days."

Dreamed it; no doubt. And dreamed the old days as well: doubtless.
Another fast dreamer. . .
                              At last we arrive at the shack.

Here's Uncle Chaos come to meet me halfway!
                                        Seems so:
Near the house an antique car is racing into the ground
And releasing its onetime overpriced atoms into the void
At the speed of rusty light.
                                   Over the doorway a splintering
Rack of flinty deer horns starts no fires in this wind.
Hung from the wall, abandoned gear goes into the weather:
Worn spurs and rotting saddles and bridles
                                                emblems
Of the gone days.
                        Indoors, deerskins cover the floors,
The bed, the few chairs.
                              There's a new shotgun.
                                                 A rifle
My father gave him — 25-20 Winchester brushgun.
Traps, snares, spears and fishing tackle: the illegal
Net. . .
          Ground zero
                        Bill Dee
                                    at home on the wind,
Adrift and at home in the universe
                                    alone. . .
                                                alive. . .

                                        And the others —
I think of Tiger Good in his shack on the Maple River
Trapping and hunting his way through the big freeze of the Thirties;
Of the squatters in Troop Number Nine's log cabin here on the Sheyenne;
Of that nameless one who lived as a hermit here in the Hills;
And of Moonlight John: his home a de-mounted twodoor carbody
Beside route 46.

Froze to death there in a three day blizzard:
Winter of the blue snow. . .
                              mavericks
                                    loners
                                         free men
And what's to show for it?
                    For Bill Dee in winter a treeful
Of moonlight.
            The snow and the river.
                              The lonely meatroads he follows
Tracking illegal dear.
                  Feuds with gamewardens.
                                      And in summer
Forty acres of butterflys fenced by verticle sun.

Now: mackerel sky: the cloudy bones of the wind;
Slow air climbing the light and the little stair
Of dustmote, waterdrop, iceflake   weightless celestial blue. . .
Nights with the winter moon caught in the stars far
Houses. . .
          And noon blazing cold in its cage of fire. . .

* * * * * *

"Seems like it was right here somewhere—place we went wrong."
—And the voice of the dead fisherman (still then alive in the future!)
Tears at my ear, at my heart, like a mad bird screaming
Or keening ghost. . .)
                  Lost. . .
                        Sunk with all hands. . .
                                          Here.
Somewhere. . .
          My grandfather saw the beginning and I am seeing
The end of the old free life of this place—or what freedom
There was: the round song at least: the solidarity
In the circle of hungry equals.

          Or if there was nothing else —
Resistance. . .
          And of Bill Dee and those others. . .
                        survivors merely,
Anachronistic.
          Nothing to build on there, though they keep
(Still!) the living will to endure and resist.
                   Alone.
Alive.
    Outlaws.
          Riding a cold trail.
              Holy. . .

              *   *   *   *   *   *

If New York holds history locked in its icy museums
                          stony
Keeps no wind can shift or shake
                  its falling walls
Spalling
        unspelling the rebel names while the prisoners sleep
In the night rock. . .
              If Los Angeles' windless calm is only
End of the continental drift
             decaying granite
                   no house
Will stand
        and change *there* merely the empty alternatives ranging
The sounding void. . .
            then what star steers and stands, what mansion
Founded on fire brightens towards us   what sea will call us
Saying: here is the road to the ancient and future light?
Exhaust these four: what's left?
             Nothing.
               Nothing?

Man is the fate of his place, and place the fate of the man
And of time
                    A beginning then
                                to know one's place.
                                                    At least
That.

                                    4.
Where.   From.   Toward.   To which.   In which.   Away from.
Into.   In.   Out of.   There.   Anywhere.   Nowhere.
(A grave step in the wrong direction.)   Here.   Where else?
Was.   Am.   Will be.   (A grave step in the right
Direction.)   (In Eden there was no place.)   (No place *else*.) Name
Sake.   Name place.   Name fake.   No
Place. Noplace: like home.   No.   No homeplace.

Wherever I'm at, you'll find me someplace close to the Front.

Here.   What-Was-Before.   What-Comes-After.   Now.
Hither, Thither & Yon: the local gods.   Being.
Becoming.   Having been. . .
                            Sherry (on the Frontier)
                                            Bourbon
(On Rye) (King of Kentucky) address:
                                Avenida Salsipuede,
Sauvquipeutville
                West Nowhere
                            Dakota
                                    Nem Mokodik
Utcha
        Texicola
                    Estados Unidos por Nada.
                                            here
(Where-the Dead Are: someplace-close-to-the-Front)
                                                Here

                            203

5.

In the pastures, now, the grass is eating the horse that time rode
(So slowly!) from between my legs and into the flowering earth. . .

Men have pastured wheat in the sun—and I was once a wheat herder—
And alas, in the richest city in the world, hunger is *free*. . .

Footsteps in stony silence. . .
                                                        is it a dream that I see
In spring the grass greener in the shape of a horse, the quick shade
Of the deer in the fading flowers in the roadside ditch where a car
Laid her?

      All things are doorways: all things are passing
And opening into each other always. . .
                                                        our housedoor equally
On Crazy Horse and the Cadillac.   (Echo of revolution
In the north 40. . .)

              But the Wobbly's footprint there led only
To crowded jails in the nameless towns. . .
                                                        And the Communists blazed trails
To Federal Pens. . .
                  But now they have superhighways for *all* of us—
Night courts, day courts—and finally, friends: *to the Wall*!

Hawks. Skulls. Skull-trumpets easy under the wind. . .
All's well.
                  I am here in the middle of my life (Or more likely
Toward the end)
                  I tally the winter count.

                    The more
The snow falls, the more my heart feels empty. The snow
Is good for the coming crops but bad for my soul. The falling

Barometer of my spirit is good for nothing
                                        still
                                    I'm *here*
And I have to be here: or elsewhere: so
                            —here for a while—
(In the economy of suffering, nothing is lost)
                                        —here.

                                        And it's only
The nostalgia for the living dead and for abandoned places that moves me.
(America is terribly old, saith the poet: Jim Wright)
Aye.
      Because nothing endures.
                            Marsh Street
                                    the Indians
                                        —gone under
The pluralistic concrete where the new freeway blinds through.

All's drift and dream.
                        Here stood a happy house,
Once: one blink of the eye and it's lost.
                                    Our whole history
Seems only a simple catalogue of catastrophe leading here. . .

But, at least: here.
                    (East is the death journey and West
The Oregon Trail to the dead myth.)
                                At least
                                        here
(Dakota the farmhouse)
                        —begun before Easter—
                                            at least
                                                at least
Here. . .

6.

The ghosts, the glory and the agon: gone.

                                      Having no past,

But only successions of failures in labor love and rebellion—
Cold-decked, the dream-pack switched by the tin-horn of the status quo—
Forward! Having no history, on to create the legend!

The tracks of a million buffalo are lost in the night of a past
Lit only by the flare of a covered wagon

                                  a harp of flesh

Is silenced

                 the book of feathers and moonlight is closed

                                            forever

On exhausted roads spun out of acetylene lamps of the dead
Overlands

               the transcontinental locomotive is anchored in concrete
Next to the war memorial

                           under the emblems of progress
A vision of April light is darkened by absent eagles. . .

It is not *my* past that I mourn—*that* I can never lose—
(Nor my future, which is assured, and in which I sing more cold
And passionate still as the passing years swing over my deadheading
Mortal part

                    heart at home on the wind

                                  borne

In the blood of strangers. . .

                         carried

                                 forward forever

                                       this song. . .)

—No, but the past of this place and the place itself and what
Was: the Possible; that is: the future that never arrived. . .

                  *   *   *   *   *   *

It is almost finished. . .
                    —the kachina.
                                    Midnight has flooded the coulee
With ancient brightness
                south
                        toward the hooded river
                                        toward the dead
And the wind is spelling a tale in the spooled snow. . .
                                        in the sea. . . .

Genya stirs in her sleep.
                    The ghosts home on my light.
We wait: the Eternal Couple: the Fool
                        the Woman
                                and the Moon. . .

VI

1.

_____and always halftime at The Funeral—but once, in Samsara. . .
That is: NOW—start in the empty anytime: arrive
Ahead of time: HERE: in the filledup nowhere, and go
FORWARD

      —"Cain't hear you boy—ain't no color but the night
Down here—get out in the stream and *sing*!
                Who be ye?"

'Tis only myself. . .
        the last man of the century. . .

                      going
Home. . .

    "Who you talk to then?
               Dark here; caint see
You."

    I'm just a worn piece of leather that was once well put together.
                        I am
The one who has come at last to wake the reluctant dreamer
Out of his surfeit of continental sleep
               to free the Bound Man
Of the Revolution
        to make your jawbone book and heavenly
Credit card.
      Sunrise in the rock. . .
            the light of my house
Burning. . .

Do you read my blaze
                   down
                              there
                                   in the dark?
                                        Over.

"Ah — that old resurrection man!
                         Talk like you found it —
Place you get out.
                But my foot
                         — stuck here in the stone. . ."

In the time it takes to make one step is the life of my poem.
And unless the step is endless, hell is forever.
                                        But hell
Shakes at one step; shatters.
                         It is *not* daybreak
Provokes cockcrow but cockcrow drags forth the reluctant sun   not
Resurrection that allows us to rise and walk but the rising
Of the rebel dead founds resurrection and overthrows hell.

                         2.
What I am doing
                ain't nobody
                         nowhere
                              done before. . .

Have come a long way and arrive tired, the feet
Of language: raw: trailworn: needing to be reshod,
And myself with saddle sores from the long night ride.
I arrive near death, near the stall of silence. . .
                                   but that's no matter —
What began in the first blaze — despair — is to end in joy:
After showing you hell I'm to blaze you the trail to heaven. . .

210

Arrive cold—after·the long fall into
The past that must be the future the future that is my past.
I see the bus go by advertising DOGMA and the blind
Veteran asking bread in the cold teeth of the night O
Ancient Witness
                    —and all unchanged in the time of this poem. . .

All to be changed.
                    I offer as guide this total myth,
The legend of my life and time.
                              But the message arrives from far off:
From some future galaxy—arrives very fast, very faint, in a language
I can barely translate. . .
                         and always the danger of shortfall, noise,
And the plaindamn inability of readers to know good sense and song. . .

And so—nights of waiting for a single word and nights
When all arrives at once like a migration of birds.
Days when I turn it off in order to breathe, days
When only an enigmatic phrase comes through from another galaxy—
Poem
        —nights. . .
                    when I am only food for the moon. . .

But hang-ups are no substitute for real agony.
                                        And I
Am born every morning. . .
                        And once
                                in Samsara
                                        and the ceremony done. . .
—Warped and bandaged arc of a broken bow I am bent
On straitening. . .

                            3.
Begun before Easter of a different year. . .Skyros. . .Dakota
The world:

                    outside my window
                                        changed and unchanged.
                                                            I have come
Back toward the light
                            (my brothers' houses all burned this year)
                                                                toward
Morning.
                    Beyond my window the armless windmills are marching
Into the sea.
                    And the iron poet strides over
The dark village.
                            Cockcrow. . .
                                    —and always springtime in Hell. . .

                            *   *   *   *   *   *

I have come here—too young for this world and too old for the next—
From my violent acres crying for incarnation, to claim you,
To found our hungry legend in the field of bread, to find
Our bread in the bank of hunger, in the lame streets of the dawn,
To find our sign past sleep or these sleepy reveries of an insomniac Harp. . .

____have come to claim you, to build, on the angry winds of the renegade
Angels, the four blueblowers of the compass points, this stand
For the round song and the commune;
                                    in the moon of bad weather to build

The pure rock of this passage   oasis of song in the cold

And desert night. . .
                            (first the stars and the sea, now
The rock and the wind)
                            —have brought you here: beyond the four
Elements: stripped: naked for travelling. . . (the dead fly *up,*
Having lightened load, through the rock. . .)

                                212

                                        Now: all the trails are blazed:
The evidence is given, the Fisherman is rising, the Kachina is made—
The ceremony is done.
                        —Now only the incantation.
                                                        I confidently wait
Your rising.
            Night, pure crystal,
                            coils in my ear
                                        like
                                        song. . .

                                4.
Begun before Easter. . .
                    Sign of the Fish. . .
                                        wind whining
Out of the black north's cold quadrant, the moon
Glistening on the folds of the coulee snow and a far scar
Where the river sings and ceases, locked in its house of ice;
Cold front sliding in: a wisp of high cirrus
Rides over the Indian graves, the barometer drowses, the burning
Clock of midnight turns on its axle of darkness. . .

                                    Had come there,
To that House, first sign in the blessed zodiac
Of all my loves and losses. . .
                        · · —to sing and summon you home.

                *   *   *   *   *   *

Now: the wind shifts
                    a star
                        falls in the sea.
Skyros
        the statue of Brooke on the citadel.
                                    Time interposes
A discontinuous strata, the sediments of the summer:

                213

What was and what is slide along old fault lines, history
Condenses its marble heros
                            a metamorphic palimpsest
Hardens between the farmhouse and here: and I dive
Into the nightrock
                    terror

                        Now I call you:
                                    I call
You:
        from the four Winds and from Fire, come forth now
My thunderbird jawsmiths and soapbox phoenixes;
                                        out of the ice-lined
Rolling coffins of the U.P. Line: rise;
                                I call you
From Water;
                blind marble of those tolling bones
Walk home forever now from the cold dismembering sea;

I call you from holy Earth:
                        boneflower: starform
                                        I call you now:
Goddess, sweet land I love, Old Lady, my darling ones —
Come:
        We'll walk up out of the night together.
                                    It's easy. . .
Only:
        open your eyes. . .
                            slip your foot out of the stone. . .
I'll take you. . .
                my darlings, my dear ones. . .
                                    over the river.

        North Dakota-Skyros-Ibiza-Agaete-Guadalajara, 1968